A scene from the Whidbey Island Center for the Arts production of *The School for Scandal.*
Left to right: Damien Cortez, Deana Duncan, George Henry, Shelley Hartle and K. Sandy O'Brien.

THE SCHOOL FOR SCANDAL

BY RICHARD BRINSLEY SHERIDAN

ADAPTED FOR CONTEMPORARY
AUDIENCES BY LEWIS JOHN CARLINO

★

DRAMATISTS
PLAY SERVICE
INC.

THE SCHOOL FOR SCANDAL
Copyright © 2004, 2005, Lewis John Carlino

All Rights Reserved

For Jill, whose Anglo-Saxon presence in my life kindled the kinship with my dear and esteemed friend Richard.

ACKNOWLEDGMENTS

This adaptation would not have been possible without the unstinting support of the staff of the Whidbey Island Center for the Arts of Langley, Washington, and their Board of Directors, and without the tireless energies of onstage and backstage crews, the scores of community volunteers, musicians, painters, set builders, and a brilliant, dedicated cast, whose faith and forbearance, through all the added rehearsals and the endless drafts and changes of text, right up to opening night and beyond, defies description. My deep and ever-abiding gratitude to all of you.

—LJC

PRODUCTION NOTES

SET MECHANICS

The design of the original production at the Drury Lane Theater, London, in 1777, was followed. However, due to a stage with less depth, the scale was reduced and two tiers of moving flats were used instead of three.

The flats that came together upstage measured eight feet wide by ten feet high. The left and right stage ones measured six feet wide by ten feet high.

Each set was composed of four painted panels: twenty-four in all for the six sets. The panels were hand-painted in bright pastel colors with perspective, dimensionality, all rendered in vivid detail.

Frames for the panels, measuring twice the dimension of their width, (to accommodate sliding them off and onstage), contained a series of tracks that ran inside the top and bottom of the frames. The bottoms of these tracks were lined with nylon strips to facilitate easy movement and to avoid jamming.

Screw eyes were inserted in the edges of the panels to which long plastic poles were attached, allowing four stagehands to synchronously move them off and onstage. This system resulted in a smooth, effortless flow of brief changes, which were very effective and elicited applause from delighted audiences.

The doors, downstage left and right, were practical and opened out and upstage.

SET-DRESSING CHANGES

The servants who had roles in the play changed the furniture and props for each scene. They were augmented with additional servants, in costume, so that this could be accomplished in the shortest time possible.

Under the able hand of the stage manger, Ms. Mannette Merrill, set pieces flowed off and onstage from closets and hallways, chair and settee coverings were changed, flowers and paintings appeared and were put into place, along with glasses, decanters, books, etc. The comings and goings of the servants were carefully choreographed and, combined with the graceful movement of the changing panels, transformed the scene changes into part of the entertainment. All the staging was unhurried, short and executed with the decorum required of well-trained servants.

To further hold the audience's interest while all this was going on, Ms Merrill's staging told a silent story for each of the servants: one servant was impatient, another tolerant, one obviously in charge, another challenging his authority, one efficient, another casual, one flirtatious, another jealous, the latter, in the last scene change of the play, finally stealing a kiss from the elusive object of his affections.

This character interplay filled the brief time between scene changes and maintained the forward movement of the play, without interruption.

MUSIC

Mr. Michael Nutt, the Music Master and leader of the Saratoga Chamber Players, along with the rest of the string quartet, played from an elaborately decorated balcony, above and right of the stage.

The music he chose for the bridges between scenes and acts was all from the period in which the play was originally performed. The selections and cues are included in the music plot of this edition.

The importance of live music in creating a wonderfully authentic ambience cannot be stressed too strongly for this play.

LANGUAGE AND MOVEMENT

Because it was difficult for the actors to uniformly master English accents, it was decided the best course to follow was for all to speak carefully enunciated standard American diction. Fortunately, the structure and rhythms of Sheridan's language were able to convey the period and culture quite effectively.

As to movement: It was found that when the actors put on their 18th-century costumes, wigs and accoutrements, they seemed quite naturally to assume the persona of the character and to be able to execute the appropriate gestures and movements of the period without a great deal of direction.

In my experience "dressing up" for the part accomplishes a great deal of physical character work for the actor, and my advice is to get them in costume and have them work with props as early in rehearsals as possible.

—LJC

This adaptation of *The School for Scandal* was originally produced by Whidbey Island Center for the Arts (Stacie Burgua, Executive Director; Deana Duncan, Production Director) in Langley, Washington, opening on April 16, 2004. It was directed by Lewis John Carlino. The cast was as follows:

FACTOTUM / SIR HARRY BUMPER .... Keith Mack
LADY SNEERWELL .... Shelley Hartle
SNAKE .... Robert Sneed
SERVANT TO LADY SNEERWELL .... Dwight Zehm
JOSEPH SURFACE .... Tom Harris
MARIA .... Bristol Branson
MRS. CANDOR .... K. Sandy O'Brien
CRABTREE .... George Henny
SIR BENJAMIN BACKBITE .... Damien Cortez
SIR PETER TEAZLE .... David Ossman
ROWLEY .... Terry Rose
LADY TEAZLE .... Deana Duncan
SIR OLIVER SURFACE .... Kirk Prindle
GEORGE (SERVANT TO SIR PETER) .... Peter Bennett
MR. PREMIUM .... Brian Plebanek
CHARLES SURFACE .... Eric Mulholland
CARELESS .... Orson Ossman
FIRST GENTLEMAN .... Charles Bieber
SECOND GENTLEMAN .... Craig Sobottka
TRIP (SERVANT TO CHARLES S.) .... Don Copeland
WILLIAM (SERVANT TO JOSEPH S.) .... Mike McVay
MAID TO LADY TEAZLE .... Nora Goodall

SARATOGA CHAMBER PLAYERS QUARTET

Music Master/Violin	*Violin*	*Violin*
Michael Nutt	Peggy Bardarson	Talia Marcus
Viola	*Viola*	*Cello*
Linda Morris	Kat Fritz	Marion Turner

Scenic/Costume/
Makeup/Wig Design
Sherri Brady

Stage Manager
Manette Merrill

Costumes
Sherri Brady
Deana Duncan
Jan Stumpf

Set Dressing
Jo Shelver
Dee Beonish
Martha Martin

Production Intern
Leah Green

Lead Painter
Diane Wilson-
simon

Scenic Painters
Chris Spencer
Emily MacArthur
Jim Troxel
Jim Scullin
Dale Boose
Leah Green
Jim Shelver
Jo Shelver
Richard Evans
Oceana Sharp
Norma Solomon

Prop Designers
Don Copeland
Jim Shelver

Props
Don Copeland
Deana Duncan
Jill Carlino
Julie O'Brien
Jo Shelver
Jim Shelver
Jim Scullin

Scenic Painters
Mears Aubin
Katrina DiNicola
K. Sandy O'Brien
Ramsey O'Brien
Manette Merrill
Abbey Duck
Shelley Hartle
David Gignac
Kimberly Hawks
Alice Sterling
Dick Edwards
Kathleen Landel
Wendy Lagerstrom
Walker Landel
Gay Bitts
Ryan Cribbs
Melanie Lowey

Music Master
Michael Nutt

Accessory Designer
Jill Carlino

Light Board
Operator
Manette Merrill

Assistant Stage
Managers
Kathy Stanely
Julie O'Brien
Theresa Piatanesi

Technical Director
Adam Michard

Set Construction
Chris Spencer
Jim Troxel
Dale Boose
Jo Shelver
Jim Shelver
Jim Scullin
Dwight Zehm
Wyatt Jarvis
Sally Spencer
Cordy Michard
Oceana Sharp
Shelley Sharp

9

CHARACTERS

FACTOTUM

SIR HARRY BUMPER

LADY SNEERWELL

SNAKE

SERVANT TO LADY SNEERWELL

JOSEPH SURFACE

MARIA

MRS. CANDOR

CRABTREE

SIR BENJAMIN BACKBITE

SIR PETER TEAZLE

ROWLEY

LADY TEAZLE

SIR OLIVER SURFACE

GEORGE (SERVANT TO SIR PETER)

MR. PREMIUM

CHARLES SURFACE

CARELESS

A GENTLEMAN

TRIP (SERVANT TO CHARLES S.)

WILLIAM (SERVANT TO JOSEPH S.)

MAID TO LADY TEAZLE

IN ADDITION:

SERVANTS ATTENDING TO
THE CHANGING OF THE SCENES

PLACE

London, England.

TIME

The 18th century.

SNAKE. ... Everyone knows you can do more with a word or look than others can with the most lurid of details.

LADY SNEERWELL. Go, you are partial and too kind, Mr. Snake. I cannot deny the satisfaction I get from spreading slander. Wounded myself, at a tender age by the envenomed tongue of scandal, I have known no pleasure equal to reducing others to the level of my own reputation.

SNAKE. *(Pouring himself a cup of tea.)* Nothing could be more natural.

—*The School for Scandal*, Act One, Scene 1

THE SCHOOL
FOR SCANDAL

Prologue

The Factotum enters from stage right, with his court staff. He walks downstage center as the overture plays, faces the audience, then strikes the floor with his staff. The music continues. Annoyed, he strikes the floor, harder. The music ends raggedly.

FACTOTUM.
  A school for Scandal? Tell me, I beseech you,
  Needs there a school this deadly art to teach you?
  Is our dear author so young to think that *he*
  Can stop the growing tide of gossipry?
  This monster, so strong and swift, will not bear gagging.
  Cut Scandal's head off, still the tongue is wagging.
  So once again our Don Quixote draws his pen,
  And seeks the demon, Scandal, in his den.
  To fight ... that's *write*, what's false or true,
  'Till every drop of blood, (that's *ink*) is spilt ... for you.
(He flourishes, makes leg, and exits, stage right. Music resumes until entrance of actors.)

ACT ONE

Scene 1

Lady Sneerwell's dressing room — mid-morning. A tea table with full service sits next to Lady Sneerwell's dressing table, upon which are a hand mirror, bottles of perfume, and make-up articles. A table with her wig and jewelry box is stage left. A small couch is stage right. Lady Sneerwell and Mr. Snake enter. Lady Sneerwell holds several hand written articles.

LADY SNEERWELL. These articles for the paper were all published?

SNAKE. They were, madam. I copied them myself, in a forged hand, so there could be no suspicion as to their origin.

LADY SNEERWELL. And did you circulate the report of Lady Brittle's sordid affair with Captain Boastall, as well?

SNAKE. In great detail. It should reach Mrs. Clackitt's ears within twenty-four hours.

LADY SNEERWELL. *(Sitting at her dressing table.)* Ah, dear Mrs. Clackitt. She has a considerable talent, don't you think?

SNAKE. Indeed. She has been the cause of six broken marriages, three sons being disinherited, four separations, and two divorces, but she lacks the subtlety that distinguishes your ladyship's little embroideries. Everyone knows you can do more with a word or look than others can with the most lurid of details.

LADY SNEERWELL. Go, you are partial and too kind, Mr. Snake. I cannot deny the satisfaction I get from spreading slander. Wounded myself, at a tender age by the envenomed tongue of scandal, I have known no pleasure equal to reducing others to the level of my own reputation.

SNAKE. *(Pouring himself a cup of tea.)* Nothing could be more natural. But there is one matter in which you have employed me that I still cannot fathom with regard to your motives.

LADY SNEERWELL. Ah, you mean with respect to Sir Peter

Teazle, and his ward, Maria?

SNAKE. I do. Now here are two brothers. Joseph Surface is apparently an admirer of your ladyship, and Charles, his younger brother, the most dissipated, extravagant, young rake in the kingdom, seems attached to Maria who clearly loves him. Therefore, I am completely mystified why you do not accept the passions of Joseph and are so eager to destroy the relationship that exists between Charles and Sir Peter's ward.

LADY SNEERWELL. I will unravel the mystery for you, my dear Snake, and tell you there is not the least passion between Mr. Joseph Surface and me.

SNAKE. I am amazed, madam! I thought …

LADY SNEERWELL. Joseph's *real* attachment is to Maria or more accurately, her *fortune*. But, as his brother Charles strongly holds her affections, Joseph is obliged to seek my assistance in snatching her away from him.

SNAKE. And of what interest is it to you whether he succeeds or not?

LADY SNEERWELL. Heavens, how dull you are, Snake! Can't you guess? It is Charles, that bankrupt in fortune and reputation, for whom I am really scheming. I would sacrifice everything for his love. *Everything!*

SNAKE. I see. How very clever of you.

LADY SNEERWELL. The plot serves our mutual interests. Joseph is a selfish, and utterly despicable knave. He poses as a model of prudence and benevolence to Sir Peter and all his friends, and with this deception has gained Sir Peter's support for his scheme to marry Maria. And Charles, my dearest Charlesn has not a friend in the house except that silly, witless, girl. So, it is she against whom we are planning our attack. *(Enter Servant to Lady Sneerwell, from stage right.)*

SERVANT. Mr. Joseph Surface.

LADY SNEERWELL. Show him in. *(Exit Servant.)* He comes every day at this time so people will take him for my lover. *(Enter Joseph Surface, from stage right.)*

JOSEPH SURFACE. My dear Lady Sneerwell, how do you do? *(Making a leg.)* Mr. Snake, your most obedient. *(Snake returns the leg.)*

LADY SNEERWELL. I have just been informing Mr. Snake of our mutual interests.

JOSEPH SURFACE. Have you, *indeed?*

LADY SNEERWELL. Yes. He has been very useful to us and I believe my confidence in him is not misplaced.

JOSEPH SURFACE. Madam, it is impossible for me not to admire a man of Mr. Snake's sensibility and discernment.

LADY SNEERWELL. Spare us the compliments. When did you last see Maria or what is more important to me, your brother, Charles?

JOSEPH SURFACE. I have not seen either since I left you, but I can report they never meet anymore. Your stories about him have taken the desired effect on the girl and have driven the wedge deeper between them.

LADY SNEERWELL. Splendid! Wonderful! My dear, precious Snake, the credit of this belongs to you and your articles. *(To Joseph.)* And do your brother's distresses increase?

JOSEPH SURFACE. With every hour. *(He picks up her hand mirror and admires his reflection.)* He is virtually insolvent, yet his dissipation and profligacy continue to exceed the imagination.

LADY SNEERWELL. Poor, dear Charles.

JOSEPH SURFACE. Yes. I wish it were in my power to be of service to him: "For the man who does not share in the distresses of a brother, even though merited by his own misconduct, deserves ... "

LADY SNEERWELL. Oh, please *don't*, Joseph. You forget you are among friends.

JOSEPH SURFACE. *(He puts the mirror down and crosses to the couch.)* True. Sorry. I'll save that one for Sir Peter. *(Sounds offstage right.)*

SNAKE. Here's company coming. I'll go and copy that other most important letter I mentioned to you. *(Making a leg.)* Mr. Surface, your most obedient.

JOSEPH SURFACE. *(Returning the leg.)* Sir, your very devoted. *(Exit Snake, stage left.)* You should not put any further confidence in that rogue.

LADY SNEERWELL. Why not?

JOSEPH SURFACE. I have lately seen him meeting with old Rowley, who was formerly my father's steward and who, as you well know, has always been my enemy.

LADY SNEERWELL. You think Mr. Snake would betray us?

JOSEPH SURFACE. Without hesitation. That knave hasn't virtue enough to be faithful even to his own villainy. Ah, Maria! *(Enter Maria, from stage right, in a rush and greatly agitated.)*

LADY SNEERWELL. Maria, sweet Maria, how do you...? Why, what's the matter, my dear?

MARIA. That fop, Sir Benjamin Backbite, has just called at Sir Peter's with his odious uncle. I had to slip out and run here to escape them.

18

LADY SNEERWELL. But what has Sir Benjamin done that you should avoid him so?

MARIA. Oh, he has *done* nothing, but 'tis for what he has *said*. His conversation is nothing more than a perpetual slander of all his acquaintances.

LADY SNEERWELL. Nay, Maria, we must make allowances, dear heart. Sir Benjamin is a wit and a poet.

MARIA. For my part, madam, I cannot tolerate wit when I see it in company with malice. Don't you agree, Mr. Surface?

JOSEPH SURFACE. Most certainly, dearest Maria. "To smile at the jest that plants a thorn in another's breast, is to become a principal in the mischief."

LADY SNEERWELL. Oh, tosh! One cannot be witty without a *little* malice. It's what makes the barb stick. *(Re-enter Servant from stage right.)*

SERVANT. Madam, Mrs. Candor is below and asks if your lady-ship's at leisure.

LADY SNEERWELL. Beg her to walk in. *(Exit Servant, stage right.)* Now, Maria, here is a character more to your taste. Though Mrs. Candor is, well ... a little talkative, everybody knows her to be the best-natured sort of woman.

MARIA. Indeed, and with her good nature and benevolence, she does more mischief than all the slings and arrows of Sir Benjamin and his uncle, Crabtree.

LADY SNEERWELL. Hush. Here she is. *(Enter Mrs. Candor, from stage right.)*

MRS. CANDOR. My dear Lady Sneerwell, how have you been this century? Mr. Surface, what news do you hear? Though indeed it is no matter, for I think one hears nothing but scandal.

JOSEPH SURFACE. Indeed, ma'am. Just so.

MRS. CANDOR. Oh, Maria, child, I heard the whole affair is off between you and Charles? His extravagance, I presume. The town talks of nothing else.

MARIA. I am very sorry the town has so little else to do.

MRS. CANDOR. So true, but there's no stopping people's tongues. I was also distressed to hear that your guardian, Sir Peter, and Lady Teazle, are not as *harmonious* as could be wished?

MARIA. 'Tis grossly impertinent for people to talk so.

MRS. CANDOR. *(Crossing to the tea table and pouring a cup of tea.) Dreadful!* Utterly shameful. And tale-bearers are as bad as the tale-makers. But how can one prevent people from talking? *(Lady*

Sneerwell crosses to the table, stage left, and puts her wig on.)

JOSEPH SURFACE. Ah, Mrs. Candor, if only everyone had your forbearance and good nature!

MRS. CANDOR. Dear Mr. Surface, I just cannot *bear* to hear people attacked behind their backs. By the by, I hope 'tis not true that your brother is absolutely ruined?

JOSEPH SURFACE. I am afraid his circumstances are very bad, ma'am.

MRS. CANDOR. *(Taking a biscuit.)* Well, you must tell him to keep up his spirits. Lord Spindle and Sir Harry Bumper are all in the same boat, I hear. So, if Charles is undone, he'll at least find some consolation in knowing that half his friends are destroyed as well.

JOSEPH SURFACE. I am sure that would be a large comfort to him, ma'am. *(Re-enter Servant. From stage right.)*

SERVANT. Mr. Crabtree and Sir Benjamin Backbite. *(Servant exits, stage right.)*

LADY SNEERWELL. Maria, your lover pursues you. You positively can't escape. *(Enter Crabtree and Sir Benjamin Backbite, from stage right, each making leg.)*

CRABTREE. Lady Sneerwell, I kiss your hands. *(Lady Sneerwell extends her hands, but Crabtree does not kiss them.)* Ah, Mrs. Candor, I don't believe you are acquainted with my nephew, Sir Benjamin Backbite? Egad, ma'am, he is a clever wit, and a pretty poet too, isn't he, Lady Sneerwell?

SIR BENJAMIN BACKBITE. Oh, fie, uncle!

CRABTREE. Nay, it's true. He is the best poet in the kingdom. Come now, no modesty

SIR BENJAMIN BACKBITE. Uncle ... please ... *really* ...

LADY SNEERWELL. I wonder that you never publish anything, Sir Benjamin.

SIR BENJAMIN BACKBITE. 'Tis exceedingly vulgar to print and, since my little *satires* are mostly of particular people, I find they circulate better by giving copies of them, in confidence, of course, to their friends. *(To Maria.)* However, I do have some love poems which, when favored by this beauteous maid, I mean to bestow on the public.

CRABTREE. *(To Maria.)* Oh, they will immortalize you! You will be handed down to posterity, like Dante's Beatrice.

SIR BENJAMIN BACKBITE. *(To Maria.)* Indeed, dear Maria. You will utterly, utterly, fall in love with them when you see them on a beautiful page, where a lovely brook of text shall meander through a meadow of margins. Gad, they will be the most elegant things of their kind!

CRABTREE. But, ladies, have you heard the news?

MRS. CANDOR. What, sir, do you mean the report of...?

CRABTREE. No, ma'am, not that one. Miss Nicely is going to be married to her own *footman!*

MRS. CANDOR. *Impossible!*

CRABTREE. Ask Sir Benjamin.

SIR BENJAMIN BACKBITE. Oh, 'tis true, 'tis true, madam. Everything is fixed.

CRABTREE. *And* they say there were pressing reasons for it.

MRS. CANDOR. Dear oh, dear. And have you heard how Miss Piper came to lose her lover and her reputation last summer at Tunbridge? Sir Benjamin, do you know the story?

SIR BENJAMIN BACKBITE. To be sure. Most entertaining.

LADY SNEERWELL. Pray *do* tell us, Mrs. Candor.

MRS. CANDOR. Well, one evening at Mrs. Ponto's supper, the conversation happened to turn on the breeding of Nova Scotia sheep. Says a young lady in the company, "Oh, I know all about that. Miss Letitia Piper, a first cousin of mine, had a Nova Scotia sheep that produced her twins." "What," cries the Lady Dowager Dundizzy — who you know is as deaf as a post — "has Miss Piper had twins?" The mistake, as you may imagine, threw the whole company into a fit of laughter. However, the next morning 'twas everywhere reported, and believed by the whole town, that Miss Letitia Piper had actually been brought to bed and delivered a pair of twins: a fine boy and girl. In less than a week there were some people who could even name the *father. (Laughter from all but Joseph and Maria.)*

LADY SNEERWELL. How delicious!

MRS. CANDOR. Mr. Surface, pray is it true that your uncle, Sir Oliver, is coming home?

JOSEPH SURFACE. Not that I know of, madam.

CRABTREE. He has been in the East Indies a deucedly long time. I expect you can scarcely remember him, eh? Sad comfort, when he returns, to hear how your brother has gone on!

JOSEPH SURFACE. *(For Maria's benefit.)* Charles has been imprudent, sir, to be sure, but he may well reform yet. I hope no busy people have already prejudiced Sir Oliver against him.

SIR BENJAMIN BACKBITE. Well, I for one, never believed him to be so *utterly* devoid of principle as people say and, though he has lost most of his friends, I am told no one is better spoken of by the *moneylenders. (Laughter.)*

CRABTREE. Yes, whenever he is sick, they get together and say prayers for his quick recovery. *(Crabtree, Sir Benjamin, and Mrs. Candor laugh.)*

JOSEPH SURFACE. *(Again, for Maria's benefit.)* This may be entertainment to you, gentlemen, but you have very little regard for the feelings of a brother.

MARIA. *(Aside.)* This is intolerable! Lady Sneerwell, I must wish you a good morning. I'm not very well. *(Maria exits, stage right.)*

MRS. CANDOR. Oh dear, she changes color very much.

LADY SNEERWELL. Do, Mrs. Candor, follow her. She may need your assistance.

MRS. CANDOR. That I will, with all my soul, madam. Poor dear girl, who knows *what* her condition may be! *(Mrs. Candor takes another biscuit and exits, stage right.)*

LADY SNEERWELL. I think she could not bear to hear Charles maligned.

SIR BENJAMIN BACKBITE. The young lady's attachment to him is obvious.

CRABTREE. But you must not let that impede your pursuit, Benjamin. Follow her and put her into good humor. Come, I'll assist you.

SIR BENJAMIN BACKBITE. Mr. Surface, I did not mean to hurt you, but depend on it, your brother is utterly undone.

CRABTREE. O Lord, yes! Undone as ever a man was. Can't raise a guinea.

SIR BENJAMIN BACKBITE. Everything sold that was movable.

CRABTREE. Not a thing left.

SIR BENJAMIN BACKBITE. And I'm very sorry also to hear other bad stories against him.

CRABTREE. Oh, yes, he has done many mean things, that's certain.

SIR BENJAMIN BACKBITE. *(Going.)* But, however, as we must be going …

CRABTREE. We'll tell you more at another opportunity. *(Crabtree and Sir Benjamin make legs and exit, stage right.)*

LADY SNEERWELL. 'Tis very hard for them to leave a subject they have not quite run to ground.

JOSEPH SURFACE. I believe the abuse was no more acceptable to your ladyship than to Maria.

LADY SNEERWELL. It was not, but what concerns me is that Maria's affection for Charles is still intact. We shall have to study the situation further. In the meantime, I'll go and plot mischief, and you, dear Joseph, shall practice virtue. Go! *(Joseph exits, stage right. Lady Sneerwell exits, stage left.)*

Scene 2

Sir Peter Teazle's parlor — shortly afterward. There are large flower arrangements everywhere. A round table with three chairs is center stage. Tables left stage, up right, and behind the couch all have vases with flower arrangements. A small couch is stage right. Enter Sir Peter Teazle, from stage left, holding a handful of bills.

SIR PETER TEAZLE. *(Outraged.)* Roses: three pounds, lilies: five pounds six, peonies ... Aghhhh! *(He comes downstage and addresses the audience, showing them the bills.)* When an old bachelor marries a young wife, what else is he to expect? 'Tis now six months since Lady Teazle made me the happiest of men, and I have been the most miserable dog ever since! A girl, born and bred in the country, who never knew any luxury beyond one plain, linen gown. And now she is slave to all the fopperies and fashions of London! She spends my fortune and contradicts me in everything. And the worst of it is, *I love her,* or I could never bear all this. Yet I'll never, *never,* be so foolish as to admit it to her. *(Enter Rowley from stage right.)*
ROWLEY. *(Bowing.)* Sir Peter, your servant. How is it with you, sir?
SIR PETER TEAZLE. Oh very bad, Master Rowley, very bad. Nothing but crosses and vexations from Lady Teazle.
ROWLEY. Come, come, Sir Peter, even if your tempers don't exactly agree, I know you love her.
SIR PETER TEAZLE. I do, but the fault is always entirely *hers!* I am, myself, the sweetest-natured man alive. I tell her that a hundred times a day!
ROWLEY. Indeed, you do.
SIR PETER TEAZLE. 'Tis maddening. And now Lady Sneerwell and that *coven* of witches that meets at her house encourage the perverseness of her disposition. And to complete the torture, Maria, my ward, over whom I ought to have the power of a father,

is determined to turn rebel too, and absolutely refuses Joseph whom I have chosen for her husband. Can you believe she *still* declares attachment for his scoundrel brother, Charles?

ROWLEY. Forgive me if I differ with you on the subject of these two young gentlemen, sir. Charles has a benevolent heart and I am convinced he will correct his errors yet.

SIR PETER TEAZLE. You are wrong, Rowley. On their father's death, as you well know, I was their guardian until their uncle, Sir Oliver made them financially independent. I had ample opportunity of judging their hearts. Joseph is a man of principle, but the other…! If Charles had inherited any grain of virtue, he has lost it with the rest of his legacy. I have never been mistaken in my *life*, Rowley. My old friend, Sir Oliver, will be deeply mortified when he finds how his generosity has been squandered.

ROWLEY. I am very sorry to find you so set against the young man, because this may be the most critical period of his life. I bring news that will surprise you.

SIR PETER TEAZLE. What is it?

ROWLEY. Sir Oliver has arrived and is, at this moment, in town.

SIR PETER TEAZLE. What? I thought you did not expect him for a month.

ROWLEY. I did not, but his passage has been remarkably quick.

SIR PETER TEAZLE. Oh, I shall rejoice to see my old friend! 'Tis sixteen years since we met. We have had so many happy days together. But does he still insist we not to inform his nephews of his arrival?

ROWLEY. Most adamantly, sir. He means to devise some test of their character.

SIR PETER TEAZLE. Oh, it won't take much effort to discover their merits. However, he shall have his way. Does he know I am married?

ROWLEY. He does, and will soon wish you joy of it.

SIR PETER TEAZLE. Nay, he will laugh at me, good Rowley. The two of us used to condemn matrimony and he has remained steadfast in his philosophy. Well, he must be soon be here. But, I pray you, not a word to him that Lady Teazle and I ever do battle.

ROWLEY. On my honor, sir, but you must be very careful not to quarrel while he is in the house with you.

SIR PETER TEAZLE. Egad, so we must. Impossible, impossible! Ah, Master Rowley, when an old bachelor marries a young wife, the crime carries the punishment along with it. Come, let us prepare for his arrival. (*Exeunt Sir Peter and Rowley, stage right.*)

Scene 3

Sir Peter Teazle's parlor — early the same afternoon. Servants add a profusion of flowers to the ones already onstage, then exit, stage left and right. Enter Sir Peter and Lady Teazle from stage left. Sir Peter almost trips over two flower baskets.

SIR PETER TEAZLE. No, no, no, Lady Teazle, I'll not bear it!

LADY TEAZLE. You may bear it or not, as you please. Though I was born in the country, I know very well women of fashion in London are accountable to no one after they are married.

SIR PETER TEAZLE. Wonderful, ma'am, delightful! So, is a husband to have no influence, no authority, whatever?

LADY TEAZLE. Authority? Good Lord, if you wanted authority over me, you should have *adopted* me, not married me. I am sure you were old enough.

SIR PETER TEAZLE. Old enough? Ay, *there* it is! Madam, though my life may be made unhappy by your temper, I tell you I'll not be ruined by your *extravagance!*

LADY TEAZLE. I am no more extravagant than a woman of fashion ought to be.

SIR PETER TEAZLE. I say again: you shall throw away no more sums on *senseless luxury! (Indicating the flowers.)* Look at all of this! You spend as much on flowers as would suffice to fill all the Houses of Parliament!

LADY TEAZLE. Am I to blame because they are so expensive in cold weather? You should find fault with the climate, not with me.

SIR PETER TEAZLE. Madam, if you had been born to it, I shouldn't wonder at this behavior, but you forget what your situation was when I married you.

LADY TEAZLE. I do not. 'Twas very disagreeable or I should never have married you.

SIR PETER TEAZLE. Yes, madam, you were living in a somewhat *humbler* style then: the daughter of just a plain country *squire. (Softening, as he looks at her tenderly.)* Do you remember when I saw you first: sitting at your knitting, in a pretty linen gown, your hair in braids, and the room hung with draperies of your own making.

25

LADY TEAZLE. Oh, I remember well the life I led: inspect the dairy and the pigs, superintend the poultry, comb my aunt Gertrud's flea-infested lapdog, and be stuck down to an old, out-of-tune, spinet to strum my father to sleep after a fox-chase.

SIR PETER TEAZLE. Yes, madam, these were the *recreations* I took you from. And now you must have your coach and three powdered footmen, and in the summer a pair of white ponies to take you to Kensington Gardens. No memory, I suppose, when you were content to ride double, behind the butler, on a castrated plow-horse?

LADY TEAZLE. It was a *mare*. Your eyesight was never much good, you poor dear.

SIR PETER TEAZLE. That was your *situation,* madam! And what have I done for you? I have made you a woman of fashion, fortune, and rank. In short, I have made you my wife!

LADY TEAZLE. Well, then, there is one more thing you can make me and that is …

SIR PETER TEAZLE. My widow, I suppose?

LADY TEAZLE. *(Aside.)* Hmnnn, there's a thought.

SIR PETER TEAZLE. Don't flatter yourself. Your conduct may disturb my peace of mind, but it shall never affect my health.

LADY TEAZLE. Oh, why do you make yourself so disagreeable and thwart me in every little expense? Would you have me be out of fashion? I should think you would like to have your wife thought a woman of taste.

SIR PETER TEAZLE. Taste? Zounds, you had no "taste" when you married me!

LADY TEAZLE. Indeed! And after *having* married you, I shall never pretend to have any again. *(She rings a bell. A maid enters, from stage left, with her hat and gloves, then exits, stage left.)* Well, now that we have finished our daily tête-à-tête, I presume Maria and I may go to our engagement at Lady Sneerwell's?

SIR PETER TEAZLE. Oh, a charming set of friends you have made there.

LADY TEAZLE. *(Putting on her hat and taking a rose from one of the arrangements.)* They are people of rank and fortune and remarkably tenacious of reputation.

SIR PETER TEAZLE. Indeed! A reputation for slandering many a poor wretch with forged tales of scandal.

LADY TEAZLE. Would you prohibit the freedom of speech?

SIR PETER TEAZLE. I would, for that lot! And they have made you just as bad as any of them.

LADY TEAZLE. Well, if 'tis so, I believe I bear the part with a tolerable grace.

SIR PETER TEAZLE. *Grace?*

LADY TEAZLE. Yes, *grace*. I bear no malice against the people I abuse. When I say an ill-natured thing, 'tis out of pure good humor; and I take it for granted they deal exactly the same with me. Well, I'm off. Good-bye to you, dearest husband. *(She leans forward and offers him her lips. Sir Peter leans forward, closes his eyes, and offers her his. Lady Teazle puts the rose between his teeth, and exits, laughing.)*

SIR PETER TEAZLE. *(Taking the rose from between his teeth and smelling it.)* With what a charming air she contradicts everything I say, and how pleasantly she shows her contempt for my authority. Even if I can't make her love me, there is, at least, sweet satisfaction in quarreling with her. She never appears as lovely as when she is doing everything in her power to plague me. *(Lord Teazle exits, stage left, smelling the rose.)*

Scene 4

Lady Sneerwell's parlor — about two P.M. A round table with three chairs is stage left. On it are a decanter and glasses. A card table with two chairs is stage right. Lady Sneerwell, Mrs. Candor, Crabtree, Sir Benjamin Backbite, and Joseph Surface, enter, from stage right.

LADY SNEERWELL. Nay, positively, we will hear it!

JOSEPH SURFACE. Yes, yes, the poem, by all means!

SIR BENJAMIN BACKBITE. Oh, plague on't, uncle! 'Tis mere nonsense.

CRABTREE. No, no. *(To the group.)* 'Twas completely extemporaneous and exceedingly clever, as you will hear! *(Ad libs: "Oh, you must. Please, etc.")*

SIR BENJAMIN BACKBITE. Oh, very well, if you utterly insist. But, ladies, you should be acquainted with the circumstance. One day last week, as Lady Curricle was taking the dust in Hyde Park in her carriage, she desired me to write some verses about her ponies, upon which, I took out my little book and in one fell swoop, produced the following: *(Reading through his lorgnette.)*

Sure never were seen two such beautiful ponies;
Other horses are clowns, but these are macaronis:
To give them this title, I'm sure can't be wrong,
Their legs are so slim, and their tails are so long.

(Enthusiastic applause from Mrs. Candor and Crabtree. The others are not so moved.)

CRABTREE. There, ladies, done in the smack of a whip, and while mounted, too!

JOSEPH SURFACE. A veritable Virgil on horseback, indeed, Sir Benjamin.

SIR BENJAMIN BACKBITE. Oh dear, sir, trifles, bagatelles ...

(Enter Lady Teazle and Maria, from stage right.)

MRS. CANDOR. I must have a copy!

LADY SNEERWELL. Maria, my love, you look grave. Come, you shall sit down to a game of whist with Mr. Surface.

JOSEPH SURFACE. Yes, come, sweet Maria.

MARIA. I take very little pleasure in cards. However, I'll do as your ladyship pleases. *(She sits and begins to play.)*

LADY TEAZLE. *(Aside.)* I am surprised Mr. Surface should sit down with her. I thought he would have taken this opportunity of speaking to me without the presence of my husband.

MRS. CANDOR. *(To Backbite and Crabtree.)* Now, I'll die; but you two have been so naughty.

LADY TEAZLE. What's the matter, Mrs. Candor?

MRS. CANDOR. They say our friend, Miss Vermilion, is not attractive.

LADY SNEERWELL. Oh, surely she is a pretty woman.

CRABTREE. I am glad you think so, ma'am.

MRS. CANDOR. Well, she has a charming fresh color.

LADY TEAZLE. Yes, when it is fresh put on. *(Laughter.)*

MRS. CANDOR. Oh, fie! Her color is natural. I have seen it come and go!

LADY TEAZLE. I dare say you have, ma'am: it goes off at night, and comes again in the morning. *(Laughter.)*

LADY SNEERWELL. Yes, yes, you must admit when Mrs. Vermillion attempts to repair the ravages of time, the results are somewhat bizarre.

SIR BENJAMIN BACKBITE. Indeed. 'Tis not that she plasters her wrinkles poorly, but that when she has finished her face, she joins it onto her neck so badly, it looks like a repaired statue on which, while the head is modern, the body's antique! *(Laughter.)*

CRABTREE. Ha, ha, ha! Well said, nephew!

MRS. CANDOR. Ha, ha, ha! Oh, how you make me laugh; but I hate you for it.

SIR BENJAMIN BACKBITE. It must be said, though, she has very pretty teeth.

LADY TEAZLE. Yes, when she is neither speaking nor laughing, which very seldom happens, for she never shuts her mouth, but leaves it always ajar, like this. *(She shows her teeth and makes a face.)*

MRS. CANDOR. *(Laughing.)* Mercy, how can you be so ill-natured?

LADY SNEERWELL. Oh, dear, Lady Teazle, I see you can be a touch severe, as well.

LADY TEAZLE. 'Tis but to do her justice.

MRS. CANDOR. Well, I for one will *never* join in ridiculing a friend, as I constantly tell my cousin Ogle, and you all know what pretensions she has about *her* beauty.

CRABTREE. To be sure! She has the oddest face I've ever seen. 'Tis a collection of features from all the points of the globe.

SIR BENJAMIN BACKBITE. So she has, indeed. The moustache of a Greek ...

CRABTREE. A Roman nose ...

SIR BENJAMIN BACKBITE. Dutchman's chin ...

CRABTREE. The hair of an Australian aboriginal. *And* each eye so adores the other, it gazes at it endlessly, thus.. *(He crosses his eyes and makes a face. General laughter.)*

MRS. CANDOR. Ha, ha, ha, ha!

LADY SNEERWELL. Come, my dears. We shall take tea and cake in the next room.

MRS. CANDOR. *(Delighted; the first one out of her chair.)* Oh, cake ... *(They start to move off.)*

SIR BENJAMIN BACKBITE. My dear, Lady Teazle, that lord of yours is certainly an odd one. I could tell you some stories about him that would make you laugh heartily if he were not your husband.

LADY TEAZLE. *(Taking his arm.)* Oh, pray don't let that stop you. Do, let's hear them all. *(Exeunt, stage left, all but Joseph Surface and Maria.)*

JOSEPH SURFACE. I see you do not approve of this behavior.

MARIA. How could I? If to make jest of the infirmities or misfortunes of those who have never injured us were deemed wit or humor, heaven grant me a double portion of dullness! Their conduct is contemptible!

JOSEPH SURFACE. I agree. To propagate scandal is wantonly malicious. But can you, Maria, feel such pity for others and have not a shred for me? Is hope to be denied my aching passion?

MARIA. Why do you distress me by renewing this subject?

JOSEPH SURFACE. Cruel girl. You would not treat me thus but I see my brother is still my rival.

MARIA. Whatever my sentiments for that unfortunate young man, I shall not feel more inclined to give him up because his distresses have lost him the regard of his brother. *(She starts to leave.)*

JOSEPH SURFACE. Nay, Maria, please … Do not leave me with a frown. *(He kneels before her, blocking her exit.)* By all that's honest, my love, I swear … *(Aside.)* Egad, here's Lady Teazle! *(Aloud to Maria.)* You must not think — no, you shall not — for, though I have the greatest regard for Lady Teazle…!

MARIA. *Lady Teazle?* What are you talking about?

JOSEPH SURFACE. But if Sir Peter were to suspect …

LADY TEAZLE. *(Aside, coming forward.)* Here's a pretty picture. *(Aloud.)* Maria, you are wanted in the next room. *(Exit Maria, stage left.)* And what is all this, pray?

JOSEPH SURFACE. She has somehow suspected my feelings for you and threatened to tell Sir Peter. I was just trying to reason with her when you came in.

LADY TEAZLE. Do you usually do your *reasoning* while walking on your knees?

JOSEPH SURFACE. *(Rising.)* Oh, she's a child, and I thought a few theatrics … But, my dearest, when are you coming to my rooms, as you promised?

LADY TEAZLE. Joseph, my pet, you must understand I accept you as a lover no further than fashion requires.

JOSEPH SURFACE. Of course, my lady: what every wife is entitled to.

LADY TEAZLE. Certainly I don't want to be out of the fashion, but I have so much of my country morality left that, though Sir Peter's temper may vex me, I don't think it would ever provoke me to …

JOSEPH SURFACE. Oh, to be sure, to be *sure*. However, if you would but ponder it, just for a moment, you would see it is the only revenge in your power.

LADY TEAZLE. Go! You are such a wicked wretch! But we shall be missed. Let us join the company.

JOSEPH SURFACE. We should not return together.

LADY TEAZLE. Yes, of course, but I advise you not to wait around for Maria. I will not permit her to come back for any more of your "reasoning", you rogue. *(Lady Teazle exits, stage left.)*

JOSEPH SURFACE. *(To the audience.)* Hmnnn. A very curious dilemma my strategies have led me into! At first, I had only wanted to ingratiate myself with Lady Teazle so she might not be my enemy with Maria, but now I see she is warming to the idea of accepting me as her lover, *de facto*. I wish I had never made such a point of establishing such a good character, for it has led me into so many plots, I must be very careful not to be exposed. *(Joseph exits, stage left.)*

Scene 5

Sir Peter Teazle's parlor, as previously seen — around four P.M. Enter, from stage right, Sir Oliver Surface, Rowley, and George, Sir Peter's servant, carrying luggage and parcels.

SIR OLIVER SURFACE. Ha, ha, ha, so my old friend, Teazle, is married, eh? And a maid from the country. Ha, ha, ha! An old bachelor so long and sunk as husband at last!

ROWLEY. Oh, you must not tease him on the subject, Sir Oliver. 'Tis a very tender point, I assure you. George, take those to Sir Oliver's chambers. *(George exits, stage left.)*

SIR OLIVER SURFACE. Poor wretch! But you say he has entirely given up on Charles and never sees him?

ROWLEY. He does not, sir, and his prejudice against him is greatly increased by jealousy with regard to Lady Teazle. A society of scandalmongers, in the neighborhood, has been unflagging in their efforts to smear his name whereas, the truth is, if the lady is, shall we say, "inclined" to one of the brothers, Joseph is the more likely.

SIR OLIVER SURFACE. Well, I will not be hasty in my judgment of Charles, I promise you. No, no, if he has done nothing false or mean, I shall forgive his extravagances.

ROWLEY. Ah, sir, it gives me new life to find that your heart is not turned against him. But here comes Sir Peter.

SIR OLIVER SURFACE. *(Crossing upstage and looking stage left.)*

Egad, so he does! Good heavens, he's greatly aged! God help the poor man, I can read husband in his face even at this distance! *(Enter Sir Peter Teazle, from stage left.)*

SIR PETER TEAZLE. Ah, Sir Oliver, my old friend! Welcome to England a thousand times!

SIR OLIVER SURFACE. Thank you, thank you, Sir Peter! I am so happy to find you well! But, what's this? You are married, eh? Well, well, since it's too late for salvation, I wish you joy with all my heart!

SIR PETER TEAZLE. Thank you, dear friend. Yes, I have entered into the ... a ... happy state, but we won't talk of that now.

SIR OLIVER SURFACE. Quite right. Old friends should not begin with regrets at first meeting. No, no, no.

ROWLEY. *(Aside, to Sir Oliver.)* Take care, sir.

SIR PETER TEAZLE. I have some excellent rare brandy. Come drink with me. Rowley, will you take a glass? *(Rowley declines.)* Sit, I pray you. *(Rowley sits on the couch.)*

SIR OLIVER SURFACE. So my nephew, Charles, is a wild rogue, is he?

SIR PETER TEAZLE. *(Pouring drinks.)* Wild? He's a lost young man, indeed, but his brother, Joseph, is what a youth should be. Everybody in the world speaks well of him.

SIR OLIVER SURFACE. Psha! Then he has bowed as low to knaves and fools as to men of honesty and virtue.

SIR PETER TEAZLE. What? Do you blame him for not making enemies?

SIR OLIVER SURFACE. Yes, if he has merit enough to deserve them.

SIR PETER TEAZLE. Nay, my friend. You'll be convinced when you know him. He professes the noblest sentiments.

SIR OLIVER SURFACE. A plague on his sentiments! If he greets me with a scrap of morality in his mouth, I shall be ill all over his carpets. *(He takes a drink)* Don't mistake me, my friend. I am not defending Charles's errors, but before I form my judgment of either of them, I intend to test their hearts. My friend, Rowley, and I have planned a little something precisely for the purpose.

ROWLEY. *(To Sir Peter.)* Indeed. For once, Sir Peter you shall see you are mistaken.

SIR PETER TEAZLE. Never! I'd stake my life on Joseph's honor! What is the gist of your scheme?

SIR OLIVER SURFACE. Well, there is this Mr. Stanley who is

nearly related to Charles and Joseph by their mother. He was once a merchant in Dublin, but has been ruined by a series of misfortunes.

ROWLEY. He has written to both Joseph and Charles for assistance. From Joseph, he has received nothing but evasive promises of future support, but Charles, on the other hand, is endeavoring to raise a sum of money, part of which, in the midst of his own difficulties, he intends for the aid of poor Stanley.

SIR OLIVER SURFACE. There, you see? Truly my brother's son.

SIR PETER TEAZLE. But how does this relate to your test?

SIR OLIVER SURFACE. Rowley will inform the brothers that Stanley has obtained permission from you to apply personally to them for help.

ROWLEY. And as neither of them has ever seen Sir Oliver since their infancy, nor Stanley, ever, Sir Oliver will assume Stanley's identity and thereby have the opportunity of judging their true natures. Believe me, sir, you will find that Charles still has, as our immortal bard expresses it, "A heart to pity and a hand open as the day, for dispensing charity."

SIR PETER TEAZLE. Bah! What good is having an open hand or purse either, when he has nothing left to give?

ROWLEY. There is more, sir. Below, awaiting Sir Oliver, is a moneylender who has done everything in his power to bring Charles to his senses with regard to his foolish extravagance.

SIR PETER TEAZLE. Well, let's have him in.

ROWLEY. *(Calling to Sir. Peter's servant.)* George, desire Mr. Premium to enter.

SIR PETER TEAZLE. And how will this moneylender assist you in this scheme?

ROWLEY. I have convinced him he has no chance of recovering the loans given to Charles but by helping Sir Oliver with his plan. *(Aside, to Sir Peter.)* I have also discovered some evidence the letters between Charles and Lady Teazle may have been forged.

SIR PETER TEAZLE. *(Aside to Rowley.)* Spare me, Rowley, I have heard too much on that subject already.

ROWLEY. Ah, here is the moneylender. *(Enter George and Mr. Premium from stage right.)*

GEORGE. Mr. Premium, sir.

ROWLEY. Mr. Premium, allow me to present Sir Oliver and Sir Peter.

MR. PREMIUM. *(Bowing, nervously.)* Your Lordships … *(Exit George, stage right.)*

SIR OLIVER SURFACE. I understand you have recently had financial dealings with my nephew, Charles.

MR. PREMIUM. I have, Sir Oliver, but the poor man was ruined well before he came to me for assistance. This very evening I am to bring to him a Mr. Farquhar, a broker and a gentleman of means. I am in hopes he will advance Charles some money.

SIR PETER TEAZLE. Charles has never borrowed from this man before?

MR. PREMIUM. No, sir.

SIR PETER TEAZLE. Egad, Sir Oliver, a thought strikes me! *(To Premium.)* You're sure Charles does not know this man?

MR. PREMIUM. Absolutely sure, sir.

SIR PETER TEAZLE. *(To Sir Oliver.)* Here is an even better opportunity of satisfying yourself than by pretending to be this poor relation, Stanley. Go with Mr. Premium as the *broker! Then* you'll see your nephew in all his glory.

SIR OLIVER SURFACE. Yes, I like this idea better! And afterwards I can visit Joseph as *Stanley!*

SIR PETER TEAZLE. Excellent! Better yet!

ROWLEY. Mr. Premium, do you understand what Sir Peter is proposing?

MR. PREMIUM. I do, sir. You may depend upon me. *(Looking at his pocket watch.)* It is near the time I was to have gone.

SIR OLIVER SURFACE. Let us be on our way, then. *(He and Premium start to exit, then stop.)* But wait! *(To Sir Peter.)* How the devil will I know what to say? There must be a language and behavior for moneylenders that I ought to know.

SIR PETER TEAZLE. Oh, there's not much to learn. Just be exorbitant enough in your demands, eh, Mr. Premium?

MR. PREMIUM. A very good point.

SIR OLIVER SURFACE. I will! I'll ask him eight or ten percent on the loan, at least.

MR. PREMIUM. Sir, if you ask no more than that, you'll be unmasked immediately.

SIR OLIVER SURFACE. What? How much then?

MR. PREMIUM. Well, if he appears not very anxious for the loan, you should ask only forty or fifty percent, but if you find him in great distress and wants the money very badly, you should ask double. Then you say you haven't the money yourself, but are forced to borrow it from a friend.

SIR OLIVER SURFACE. Right. I borrow it from a friend.

MR. PREMIUM. And your friend is an unconscionable dog, but you can't help that.

SIR OLIVER SURFACE. A wicked, unconscionable, dog.

SIR PETER TEAZLE. *(Laughing.)* I believe, "Mr. Farquhar," you'll soon be master of the trade. *(To Premium.)* Shouldn't he offer him an advance against his inheritance? That would be in character, I should think.

MR. PREMIUM. An *excellent* point, sir.

SIR OLIVER SURFACE. *(To Mr. Premium.)* Well, let us be gone. You shall give me further instructions along the way. *(Sir Oliver and Premium exit, stage right.)*

SIR PETER TEAZLE. Now I'm certain Sir Oliver will be convinced. I fear you are too loyal, Rowley, and would have alerted Charles to the plot.

ROWLEY. No, upon my word, Sir Peter.

SIR PETER TEAZLE. Well, well, go now and pursue the matter of those letters between Charles and Lady Teazle. I see Maria and want to speak with her. *(Exit Rowley, stage right.)* I should be glad to be convinced my suspicions about Charles and my wife were unjust. I'll ask my friend, Joseph, for his advice. I know he will give me his honest opinion. *(Enter Maria, from stage right.)* So, child, has Joseph returned with you?

MARIA. No, sir. He was engaged.

SIR PETER TEAZLE. Sit. I wish to speak to you about him. *(She sits on the couch. Sir Peter sits next to her.)* Now, my dear, do you not begin to see the more you spend time with that amiable young man, the more his love for you deserves your reciprocity?

MARIA. Sir Peter, your constant harping on this subject distresses me extremely. I would prefer, nay, even give my heart to any gentleman who paid me the *slightest* attention rather than accept Joseph Surface.

SIR PETER TEAZLE. *Zounds,* you are perverse!

MARIA. That is *unkind,* sir! You know I have obeyed you in neither seeing nor corresponding with Charles. Indeed, I have heard enough to convince me that he is unworthy of my regard, yet I cannot understand how you could think to condemn me because I still feel some pity for his distresses.

SIR PETER TEAZLE. Pity him as much as you please, but resign yourself to marrying Joseph.

MARIA. *(Standing.)* Never!

SIR PETER TEAZLE. You will *not* be obstinate in this matter!

35

Take care, Maria. You have never yet known the true weight of a guardian's authority. Do not compel me to demonstrate it to you!

MARIA. Sir, you shall not have just reason. By my father's will I am bound to regard you as his substitute, but I must cease to think you so when you would compel me to be *miserable!* *(Maria exits stage left, weeping.)*

SIR PETER TEAZLE. *(Pouring himself a drink.)* Was ever man so crossed? Everyone conspires against me! I had not been married a *fortnight*, before her father, a hale and hearty man, died. On purpose, I believe, for the pleasure of plaguing me with the care of his daughter. *(He sits on the couch. Lady Teazle sings without.)* Here comes my other tormentor. Wonder of wonders: She appears in a good humor for a change. *(Enter Lady Teazle, from stage right.)*

LADY TEAZLE. Lord, Sir Peter, I hope you haven't been quarreling with Maria? I thought you saved all your bad temper for me.

SIR PETER TEAZLE. Nay, dear wife, you know you have the power to sweeten my disposition at all times.

LADY TEAZLE. I hope I have, dear husband, for I want you to be in a charming, sweet mood this very moment. Let me have two hundred pounds, will you?

SIR PETER TEAZLE. Two hundred pounds? Egad, do I not deserve to be happy without paying for it? But when you entreat me thus, there's nothing I could refuse you. You shall have it. *(He takes out the money and offers it.)* But seal me a bond for the repayment. *(He offers her his lips. Lady Teazle takes the money and offers him her hand.)*

LADY TEAZLE. My note of hand will do as well.

SIR PETER TEAZLE. *(Kissing her hand.)* Shall we always be at odds like this, my precious?

LADY TEAZLE. I would stop quarreling this very instant if you would admit it is you who always starts.

SIR PETER TEAZLE. Very well, my love, let all our future contests be which one of us shall be most obliging to the other.

LADY TEAZLE. You see, how good nature becomes you? You look now as you did before we were married, when you used to walk with me under the elms and tell me stories of what a *gallant* you were in your youth, and chuck me under the chin. Yes, you *would*. And ask me if I thought I could love an old fellow who would deny me nothing, didn't you?

SIR PETER TEAZLE. Yes, yes. You were so sweet and attentive, and …

LADY TEAZLE. Yes, I was, and would always take your part when my friends used to abuse and ridicule you.

SIR PETER TEAZLE. You did.

LADY TEAZLE. And when my cousin Sophie called you an ugly, cantankerous, old bachelor and laughed at me for thinking of marrying someone who could be my father, I have always defended you and said I didn't think you very ugly at all.

SIR PETER TEAZLE. Thank you.

LADY TEAZLE. And insisted you'd make a very good sort of a husband.

SIR PETER TEAZLE. You prophesied right. And now we shall be the happiest of couples.

LADY TEAZLE. And never differ again?

SIR PETER TEAZLE. Never. *(They kiss. A quiet moment of bliss.)* Though, seriously, you really must watch your temper. In all our little quarrels, if you remember, my honey cake, it is *you* who always begins first.

LADY TEAZLE. No, my *plum pudding*. 'Tis *you* who always gives the first provocation.

SIR PETER TEAZLE. Now, now, my angel, take care. Contradicting isn't the way to be *obliging*.

LADY TEAZLE. Then don't *do* it, my *treasure*.

SIR PETER TEAZLE. There, now, you see? You are beginning the very thing you know makes me angry.

LADY TEAZLE. Can I help it if you will be contentious without reason?

SIR PETER TEAZLE. So you *do* want to quarrel again!

LADY TEAZLE. I don't, but when you insist on being peevish …

SIR PETER TEAZLE. *Peevish? Egad,* I was just …

LADY TEAZLE. Oh, there's no bearing your temper! *(She gets up and crosses left.)*

SIR PETER TEAZLE. *(Getting up and following.)* No, no, madam, the fault's in *your* temper!

LADY TEAZLE. You are just what my cousin Sophie said you would be.

SIR PETER TEAZLE. Your cousin Sophie is a forward, impertinent idiot!

LADY TEAZLE. And you are a great, ugly, bear!

SIR PETER TEAZLE. May all the plagues of marriage be doubled on me if ever I try to be friends with you any more!

LADY TEAZLE. So much the better!

SIR PETER TEAZLE. *(Draining his glass.)* 'Tis evident you never cared a pin for me. I was a madman to marry you!

LADY TEAZLE. And I was a fool to marry *you:* an old, dangling, bachelor, who was single at fifty because he could never meet any one who would have him!

SIR PETER TEAZLE. I have *done* with you! You are unfeeling, and ungrateful. I now believe you capable of everything that is bad. Yes, *now* I believe the reports about you and Charles Surface.

LADY TEAZLE. *What?*

SIR PETER TEAZLE. Yes, madam, *you and Charles,* are not without grounds!

LADY TEAZLE. Take care, Sir Peter! You had better not accuse me of any such thing! I'll not be suspected without cause!

SIR PETER TEAZLE. Madam, you shall have your separate maintenance as soon as you please, or a *divorce,* if you like! Yes, your highness! I'll make an example of *myself* for the benefit of all old bachelors. I say let us *separate!*

LADY TEAZLE. Agreed! And now that we are of one mind again, my lovely, we may be the happiest couple, and never differ again. Ha, ha, ha! Well, I see you are going apoplectic and I don't want to interrupt you, so, ta, ta, dear relic. *(Lady Teazle exits, stage right.)*

SIR PETER TEAZLE. Plagues and tortures on all who would marry! Plagues and tortures on the lot of 'em! *(Sir Peter exits, stage left.)*

Scene 6

A dining room in Charles Surface's house — shortly following. The room is empty of furnishings except for a long table, two benches, and a chair. On the table are a number of wine bottles, some empty, some half full, two tankards, and a bowl of apples. Charles Surface, Sir Harry Bumper, Careless, and a Gentleman, enter carrying tankards and drinking. They move to the table and sit.

CHARLES SURFACE. No, no, 'tis true, gentlemen! We live in an age of *appalling* degeneracy. Many of our friends have taste, spirit, and politeness, but damn them, they don't *drink.* Isn't that so, Careless?

CARELESS. Indeed, Charles! They provide all the luxuries of the table, but abstain from wine and wit and all society suffers by it intolerably!

ALL. *(Banging their tankards on the table.)* Hear, hear!

CHARLES SURFACE. What man can pretend to be a believer in love, who does not partake of wine? 'Tis the nectar with which the lover primes his heart!

ALL. *(Laughter, ad libs.)* Hear, hear!

CARELESS. *(To Charles.)* Ah, then, what of your heart, Charles? Tell us the object of *your* deepest carnal affections?

ALL. *(Banging their tankards.)* Yes, yes!

CHARLES SURFACE. I have withheld her name only out of consideration for you, because if I toast her, you would be forced to raise your glasses to her peers, and that would be completely impossible!

CARELESS. *Bollox!* I'm sure we could find some tasty vestal virgins or heathen goddesses that would do!

ALL. *(Banging their tankards.)* Hear, hear!

CHARLES SURFACE. Well then tankards, all, *tankards!* To Maria!

ALL. Maria! Maria!

SIR HARRY BUMPER. Maria, who?

CHARLES SURFACE. Damn the surname! She does not need one to be registered in The Book of Love. I say again, Maria!

ALL. Maria! *(They raise their tankards, toast, then drink.)*

CHARLES SURFACE. Your turn now, Sir Harry Bumper. Mind you now, the toast must be to beauty unsurpassed.

ALL. *(Banging their tankards.)* Hear, hear!

CARELESS. *(To Sir Harry.)* Have not a care, Bumper. I'll second your toast, though she is bald, earless, and without chin. *(Laughter. Charles' servant, Trip, enters from stage right, evidently under the influence.)*

SIR HARRY BUMPER. Nay, I'll give you sots a song instead! *(He climbs onto the table and sings.)* "Here's to the maiden of bashful fifteen. Here's to the widow of fifty. Here's to the flaunting extravagant queen, and here's to the housewife that's thrifty."

ALL. *(Singing the chorus. Trip sings as well.)* "Let the toast pass. Drink to the lass, and I'll wager she'll prove an excuse for a glass."

SIR HARRY BUMPER. *(Singing.)* "Here's to the charmer whose dimples we prize. Now to the maid who has none, sir. Here's to the girl with a pair of blue eyes … "

CARELESS. *(Covering one eye with his hand.)* And here's to the wench with but one, sir. *(Laughter.)*

ALL. *(Singing the chorus.)* "Let the toast pass. Drink to the lass,

39

and I'll wager she'll prove an excuse for a glass." *(They bang their tankards on the table.)* Bravo! Bravo! *(Trip whispers to Charles.)*

CHARLES SURFACE. Gentlemen, you must excuse me a little. Careless, take the chair, will you?

CARELESS. What's this, Charles, one of your incomparable beauties, dropped in by chance?

CHARLES SURFACE. No, no! 'Tis Mr. Premium and a broker.

CARELESS. A *broker?* Let's have them in!

GENTLEMAN. Yes, yes, by all means!

CHARLES SURFACE. Trip, bid the gentlemen walk in.

TRIP. Yes, sir. *(Trip starts off stage left, realizes he's headed in the wrong direction, reverses course, and staggers out, stage right.)*

CARELESS. Let us be generous with the Burgundy and perhaps they'll be sympathetic.

CHARLES SURFACE. Nay, sir! Wine does but draw forth a man's natural qualities and to give them drink would only increase their knavery. *(Laughter. Re-enter Trip, from stage right, with Sir Oliver Surface and Mr. Premium.)*

TRIP. The gentlemen from the city, sir. *(He hiccoughs.)*

CHARLES SURFACE. Pray walk in, Mr. Premium. And what is this gentleman's name?

SIR OLIVER SURFACE. *(Aside, to Premium.)* I've forgotten my name!

MR. PREMIUM. *(To Sir Oliver.)* Farquhar, sir.

SIR OLIVER SURFACE. Yes, of course. *(To Charles.)* Farquhar, my good sir.

CHARLES SURFACE. You are both most welcome. Wine, Trip. *(Trip fills their tankards, sneaks a drink from the bottle, then exits stage right.)* Sit down, Mr. Premium. Sit down, sit down. Come, Mr. Farquhar. *(Raising his tankard.)* Success to moneylenders!

MR. PREMIUM. Success to moneylenders!

CARELESS. Indeed! For they are men of prudence and deserve to succeed!

SIR OLIVER SURFACE. Then here's to all the success they deserve! *(All cheer and drink. Sir Oliver takes only a small sip of wine.)*

CARELESS. No, no, that won't do, Farquhar! You must drink it all!

GENTLEMAN. Yes, and then another!

MR. PREMIUM. Oh, pray, sir, please consider Mr. Farquhar's a gentleman.

CARELESS. And therefore must love good wine.

GENTLEMAN. This is mutiny and a high contempt for the

chair! Give him the bottle!

CARELESS. Nay, a *cask!*

ALL. *(Banging their tankards.)* Hear, hear!

CARELESS. *(Grabbing a bottle.)* Yes, we'll see justice done to the last drop. *(They drag Sir Oliver across the table and try to force him to drink. In the scuffle, Sir Oliver's wig comes off.)*

SIR OLIVER SURFACE. Nay, pray, gentlemen, I did not expect to be used thus!

CHARLES SURFACE. *(Pulling them off.)* No, hang it, unhand him! Gentleman, please, Mr. Farquhar's a guest!

SIR OLIVER SURFACE. Good God, what have I gotten myself into? *(Charles retrieves Sir Oliver's wig and hands it to Premium. Premium helps Sir Oliver put it back on.)*

CARELESS. A plague on 'em! If they won't drink, we'll not sit down with them! Come, Sir Harry, the dice are in the next room. Charles, join us when you have finished your business.

CHARLES SURFACE. I will, I will! *(Exeunt, stage left, Gentleman, Sir Harry, with Careless following.)* Careless, do not leave: I may need you later.

CARELESS. At your service, sir. Always ready: word, note, or bond, 'tis all the same to me. *(He exits, stage left.)*

MR. PREMIUM. *(To Charles.)* Sir, Mr. Farquhar is a gentleman of the strictest honor and secrecy and always brings to fruition what he undertakes. He is …

CHARLES SURFACE. Oh, *stop,* Premium. *(To Sir Oliver.)* He'll be an hour giving us our titles. *(He draws up a chair for him.)* Sit here, sir. You will be more comfortable. Now, the plain state of the matter is this: I am an extravagant young fellow who wants to borrow money. You, I take to be a prudent old fellow, who has money to lend. I am blockhead enough to give fifty percent sooner than not have it! And you, I presume, are rogue enough to take a hundred if you can get it. Now, sir, you see we are acquainted at once and may proceed to business without further ceremony.

SIR OLIVER SURFACE. Sir, I see you are a man who speaks without flourish, and I like you the better for it. *(Sir Oliver puts his hand on Charles' knee. Premium clears his throat and gestures caution. Sir Oliver, realizing what he's doing, withdraws his hand.)*

CHARLES SURFACE. Well, I know money isn't to be bought without paying for't.

SIR OLIVER SURFACE. Indeed not. Now then, what security could you give? No land, I suppose?

CHARLES SURFACE. Only what you will find in those flower-pots outside the window, but are you acquainted at all with any of my relatives, sir?

SIR OLIVER SURFACE. Oh, indeed, I am.

CHARLES SURFACE. *(Taking an apple from the bowl and biting into it.)* Then you must know I have a very rich uncle in the East Indies: Sir Oliver Surface, from whom I have the greatest expectations. They tell me I am his favorite nephew and that he talks of leaving me everything.

SIR OLIVER SURFACE. Indeed? This is the first *I've* heard of it.

CHARLES SURFACE. Yes, yes, 'tis so. Mr. Premium knows 'tis true, don't you, Mr. Premium?

MR. PREMIUM. Oh, yes, I'll swear to it.

CHARLES SURFACE. I propose, Mr. Farquhar, a bond on my uncle's life, payable on his death, though it pains me to do so. The dear old fellow has been so good to me, that I truly should be very sorry to hear anything had happened to him.

SIR OLIVER SURFACE. No more then I, I assure you. However, this happens to be the worst security you could offer. Sir Oliver might live to be a *hundred*. I hear he is as hale as any man of his years in Christendom.

CHARLES SURFACE. Oh, sir, you are terribly misinformed. The climate in India has hurt him and he declines rapidly.

SIR OLIVER SURFACE. But I'm told he's coming home. Nay, some say he is actually arrived in England.

CHARLES SURFACE. *(Tossing the apple on the floor.)* Cod's wallop! No, no. At this very moment he is probably on his death bed, in Calcutta. Isn't that right, Mr. Premium?

MR. PREMIUM. Without a doubt.

SIR OLIVER SURFACE. Ha, ha, ha! Oh his death bed, you say? Well, certainly you must know better than I. I understand you want a few hundred pounds immediately. Is there nothing you could dispose of?

CHARLES SURFACE. Nothing.

SIR OLIVER SURFACE. What, nothing at *all* of the family property left?

CHARLES SURFACE. Not much, unless you would fancy the family pictures. *That's it! Yes!* I've got a room full of ancestors above, and if you have a taste for old paintings, you can have 'em at a bargain!

SIR OLIVER SURFACE. *Blast me, man,* you would sell your fore-fathers?

CHARLES SURFACE. Every man of them, to the highest bidder.

SIR OLIVER SURFACE. *Your great-uncles and aunts?*

CHARLES SURFACE. Ay, great-grandfathers and grandmothers too.

SIR OLIVER SURFACE. *(Aside.)* Now I give up! *(To Charles, forgetting himself.)* My dear sir, have you no respect for your own kindred? Odd's life! Do you take me for a *knave*, that you would raise money from me on your own flesh and blood? *(He starts to leave. Premium and Charles restrain him.)*

CHARLES SURFACE. Nay, Mr. Farquhar, please don't upset yourself. What do you care, as long as you have value for money? *(Premium nudges Sir Oliver.)*

SIR OLIVER SURFACE. What? Oh, oh, yes. Very well, I will purchase them. I think I can dispose of the family canvas. *(Aside.)* Oh, I'll never forgive him for this, *never!* *(Re-enter Careless from stage left.)*

CARELESS. What the devil is keeping you, Charles?

CHARLES SURFACE. I can't come yet. We are going to have a sale in the picture room. Mr. Farquhar is buying all my ancestors!

CARELESS. Oh, burn your ancestors! *(He starts to go off.)*

CHARLES SURFACE. No, join us, Careless. You shall be the auctioneer. Come.

CARELESS. Splendid! Going, going ... *(Laughter.)*

SIR OLIVER SURFACE. *(Aside.)* Oh, the rogues!

CHARLES SURFACE. And you, good Premium, shall be appraiser. What's wrong, Mr. Farquhar? You don't seem pleased.

SIR OLIVER SURFACE. Oh, yes, I am, vastly! Ha, ha, ha! Yes, yes, I think it a rare joke to sell one's family by auction. Ha, ha! *(Aside.)* The scoundrel! *(Charles and Careless fill their tankards, drink, then sing as they exit, stage left.)*

CHARLES and CARELESS. "Let the toast past. Drink to the lass, and I'll wager she'll prove an excuse for a glass."

SIR OLIVER SURFACE. I'll never forgive him, *never!* *(Sir Oliver and Premium follow.)*

Scene 7

*A picture room in Charles Surface's House — immediately
following. The room is bare except for a chair and a standing
desk with a quill and inkpot on it. The walls are hung with
family portraits. Several paintings lean against the desk. The
Surface family tree hangs on the wall, near the desk. Enter,
from stage right, Charles Surface, Sir Oliver Surface, Mr.
Premium, and Careless. Shouting and laughter from the dice
game, offstage left.*

CHARLES SURFACE. Walk in, gentlemen. Here they are: the
family of the Surfaces, some from the Norman Conquest.
SIR OLIVER SURFACE. Splendid, indeed. A fine collection.
CHARLES SURFACE. Ay, all rendered in their true likeness: stiff
and awkward as the originals, which resemble nothing ever seen in
nature.
SIR OLIVER SURFACE. Yes. We shall never see such figures of
elegance again.
CHARLES SURFACE. *(Aside.)* I should hope not. *(To Careless.)*
But come, get to your pulpit, Mr. Auctioneer. That standing desk
of my grandfather's will serve our purpose.
CARELESS. Ay, but I haven't a hammer, Charles, and what good's
an auctioneer without his hammer?
CHARLES SURFACE. Egad, that's true! *(Looking around.)* Ah,
this will do: our family's complete genealogy. *(He takes from the
wall the plaque on which is painted the family tree.)* Here, Careless,
here's the family tree for you! This shall be your hammer. Now you
can knock down my ancestors with their own pedigree.
SIR OLIVER SURFACE. *(Aside.)* Oh, the rogue!
CARELESS. The most perfect thing you could have found,
Charles, for 'twill not only serve as a hammer, but as a catalogue for
the auction, as well. Come, begin! A-going, a-going, a-going …
(He bangs the plaque on the desk. He and Charles laugh.)
CHARLES SURFACE. Bravo, Careless. Now then, here's my great
uncle, Sir Richard Ravelin, a great general in his day, I assure you.
CARELESS. *(Tracing the names on the family tree with his finger.)*

Ravelin ... Ah, *Ravelin!* What say you, Mr. Farquhar? A braver hero you will not find. What do you bid?

SIR OLIVER SURFACE. *(Aside to Mr. Premium.)* Ask him to name a price.

MR. PREMIUM. *(To Charles.)* Mr. Farquhar would have you say.

CHARLES SURFACE. Right. He shall have him for ... ten pounds, and I'm sure that's not too dear for a staff-officer. *(Careless nods agreement.)*

SIR OLIVER SURFACE. *(Aside.)* His famous uncle Richard for ten pounds! *(Aloud.)* Very well, sir, I'll take him at ten.

CHARLES SURFACE. *(To Careless.)* Knock down my uncle Richard.

CARELESS. *(Banging the plaque on the desk.)* Done at ten!

CHARLES SURFACE. This is a maiden sister of his, my great-aunt, Deborah, done by Reynolds, and said to be a very accurate likeness. There she is, a shepherdess with her flock. You shall have her for six pounds five. A bargain. The sheep alone are worth the money.

SIR OLIVER SURFACE. *(Aside.)* Poor Deborah: a woman who set such a value on herself! *(Aloud.)* She's mine.

CHARLES SURFACE. *(To Careless.)* Knock down my aunt Deborah!

CARELESS. *(Banging the plaque.)* Auntie sold at six pounds five shillings!

MR. PREMIUM. 'Tis a very good bargain. *(Sir Oliver nods assent. Laughter and shouting from offstage left.)*

CHARLES SURFACE. *(Indicating two portraits on the wall.)* Now these are two brothers: William and Walter Blunt, Esquires, both members of Parliament and noted speakers and what's very extraordinary, I believe this is the first time they were ever bought or sold.

SIR OLIVER SURFACE. Very extraordinary, indeed, for men in government! I'll take them at your own price, for the honor of Parliament.

CARELESS. Well said, good Farquhar! Sold at forty!

SIR OLIVER SURFACE. *Forty?*

CHARLES SURFACE. Oh, a plague on it! We shall be all day retailing in this manner. Let us deal wholesale. What say you, Farquhar? Give me three hundred pounds for all the rest of them.

CARELESS. Ay, that will be the best way.

SIR OLIVER SURFACE. Well, well, anything to accommodate you. Done! They are mine. *(Charles and Careless shake hands, congrat-*

45

ulating each other.) But there is that portrait you have passed over.

CARELESS. *(Picking up Sir Oliver's picture and looking at it.)* Yes, Charles. Who is this ill-looking little fellow?

SIR OLIVER SURFACE. *(Going to Careless.)* Sir, I do not think him so ill-looking, by any means.

CHARLES SURFACE. That's my uncle Oliver. 'Twas done before he went to India.

CARELESS. Your *Uncle Oliver?* God help you, Charles, then there's no hope for you. That's as mean and disinheriting-looking-rogue as ever I saw. Don't you agree, Farquhar?

SIR OLIVER SURFACE. *(Taking the picture away from him.)* I do not, sir! That it is as honest a looking face as any in the room, dead or alive. I'll take him with the rest.

CHARLES SURFACE. *(Taking the picture from Sir Oliver.)* No, sir, you shall not! I'll not part with dear Ollie. The old fellow has been very good to me, and, by heaven, while I've a room to put it in, I'll keep his picture.

SIR OLIVER SURFACE. *(Aside.)* The rascal's my nephew after all! *(Aloud, to Charles.)* I don't know why, sir, but I have somehow taken a fancy to that particular portrait.

CHARLES SURFACE. I'm sorry, but you cannot have it. Haven't you got enough of them?

SIR OLIVER SURFACE. *(Aside.)* I forgive him everything, *everything!* *(Aloud, taking out his check book and writing a check.)* Mr. Surface, when I like something, money is no object. I'll give you as much for that fine, *handsome,* gentleman as for all the rest of your family.

CHARLES SURFACE. No, master broker. I will not *part* with him.

SIR OLIVER SURFACE. *(Aside.)* How like his father the dog is. *(Aloud.)* Well, well, I have done. Here is a draught for your sum. *(He hands the check to him.)*

CHARLES SURFACE. *What?* Sir, this is for *eight hundred pounds!*

SIR OLIVER SURFACE. Yes. I've included Sir Oliver.

CHARLES SURFACE. *(Attempting to hand the check back to him.)* Zounds, *no,* I tell you, once and for all! And that's the end of it!

SIR OLIVER SURFACE. *(Refusing to accept the check; pushing his hand away.)* Never mind. We'll balance the difference another time. Give me your hand on the bargain. *(He shakes his hand, then, forgetting himself, embraces him.)* You are a good and honest fellow, Charles. *(Premium clears his throat. Sir Oliver releases him and steps back.)* I beg pardon, sir, for being so familiar.

CHARLES SURFACE. Mr. Farquhar, promise me you'll see my family has suitable lodgings?

SIR OLIVER SURFACE. You may rely on it. I'll send for them in a day or two.

CHARLES SURFACE. Ay, all but my dear old Ollie.

SIR OLIVER SURFACE. *(Looking at the painting.)* Yes, dear old Ollie. *(Offstage left voices, shouting and laughing.)*

CARELESS. *(Aside, to Charles.)* Charles, this is the oddest broker I've ever met.

CHARLES SURFACE. *(Aside, to Careless.)* He is the very *prince* of brokers. *(Shouts and laughter offstage, at a win.)* That sounds like a win for Sir Harry.

CARELESS. Come, now that you're rich again, let's join the game.

CHARLES SURFACE. *(To Sir Oliver and Premium.)* Gentlemen, please excuse us a moment. I will rejoin you shortly. *(Premium and Sir Oliver bow. Charles and Careless exit, stage left.)*

SIR OLIVER SURFACE. By God, now I'll drink! *(He pours wine into the two tankards left by Careless and Charles.)*

MR. PREMIUM. Well, sir, you have seen Charles in high glory, just as Sir Peter said. 'Tis a great pity he is so extravagant.

SIR OLIVER SURFACE. *(Looking at his picture.)* Yes, but he would not sell my picture.

MR. PREMIUM. ... and loves wine and women so much.

SIR OLIVER SURFACE. Absolutely refused me! *(Voices, laughing and shouting, from offstage, left.)*

MR. PREMIUM. ... and plays at dice.

SIR OLIVER SURFACE. But would not part with my beautiful picture, even though he sold the rest of his ancestors like old tapestry. Well, well, I'll pay *all* his debts, what he owes you, as well, Mr. Premium, and more, for your good services.

MR. PREMIUM. *(A gasp. Relieved and overwhelmed.)* I am most grateful, sir, for your generosity.

SIR OLIVER SURFACE. You are most welcome, Mister Premium. Ha, ha, ha. And, now that I am not longer "Farquhar" the broker, I'm off to Joseph's as poor Stanley.

MR. PREMIUM. Who is expected within the hour.

SIR OLIVER SURFACE. *(Shouts and laughter from offstage left.)* Ah, Premium, to be young again. *(Sir Oliver raises his tankard.)* To my dear, wonderful, charitable, and extravagant nephew!

SIR OLIVER SURFACE and MR. PREMIUM. To Charles! *(They drink, then Sir Oliver sings.)*

SIR OLIVER SURFACE. "Let the toast pass. Drink to the lass and I'll wager she'll prove an excuse for a glass." *(Shouts and laughter from off left.)* Sing, good Premium! Sing! *(They both exit right, singing.)*

MR. PREMIUM and SIR OLIVER SURFACE. Let the toast pass, drink to the lass, and I'll wager she'll prove an excuse for a glass. *(Charles re-enters from stage left, still holding the check.)*

CHARLES SURFACE. Gentlemen, come join us in a game of ... *(Finding them gone, he smiles, shakes his head, shrugs, then picks up the bottle Sir Harry left, and looks at the picture of Sir Oliver and the rest of his ancestors. To the audience.)* Well, it seems my ancestors are more valuable relations than I took them for! *(He bows ceremoniously to the pictures.)* Ladies and gentlemen, your most obedient and *very* grateful servant. *(Rowley enters.)* Ah, Rowley, you are just in time to take leave of your old acquaintances.

ROWLEY. I heard they were going. But how can you be in such high spirits under so much distress?

CHARLES SURFACE. Yes, 'tis all very moving, but since I want to remain in this house, and *they* never move a muscle, why should I? *(Handing him the check.)* Here, my friend. Get this changed without delay and take a hundred pounds of it immediately to old Stanley.

ROWLEY. A *hundred pounds!* But sir, there are so many other bills to be ...

CHARLES SURFACE. Gad's life, man, poor Stanley is *desperate* and if you don't make haste we shall have others pounding on my door that have a better right to the money!

ROWLEY. Charles, think for a moment. Your creditors will ...

CHARLES SURFACE. Yes, yes, I'm sure you're right, Rowley, but, by heaven, while I have, I'll give. So, damn my creditors! Be gone, I say. Be gone!

ROWLEY. As you wish, sir. *(Laughter and shouts from offstage left.)*

CHARLES SURFACE. And now for dice! *(Charles exits stage left.)*

ROWLEY. *(To the audience.)* Ha ha ha. Oh, Sir Oliver will laugh at this. How very droll: that Charles should pay Sir Oliver's benevolence back to him. Ha ha ha. *(Rowley exits, stage right.)*

End of Act One

Intermission Speech

Music begins. The Factotum enters from stage right, walks downstage, and strikes the floor with his staff. The music stops, instantly. The factotum nods to the musicians.

FACTOTUM.
My lords and ladies, 'tis time for your refreshment.
Libations, assignations, disputations and reputations
all await your pleasure and embellishments.
Ample time now to monger scandal,
And for tittle-tattle to scramble ...
Our players most humbly await your scorn or praise,
Eager to guide you further
through this entangled maze.
(He nods to the musicians. They begin to play. He makes flourish and leg, then exits. House lights up.)

ACT TWO

Scene 1

The library in Joseph Surface's House — around four P.M. A wing chair, with a table and books alongside, is stage left. Far left is another small table. Downstage right is a table with two chairs. A decanter and glasses are on the table. A table upstage right holds a number of books and a small hand mirror. A screen covered with maps is left of the table. Enter Joseph Surface and William, his servant, from stage right.

JOSEPH SURFACE. No note from Lady Teazle?

WILLIAM. No, sir.

JOSEPH SURFACE. *(Aside, to the audience.)* She should have sent one if she was prevented from coming. There may be some danger here of losing Maria through this amorous intrigue. No, no, never fear, Joseph. Charles' folly will shield you from all harm. *(Knocking without.)*

WILLIAM. Sir, I believe that must be Lady Teazle.

JOSEPH SURFACE. See whether it is before you go to the door. I have a particular message for you if it should be my brother.

WILLIAM. *(Looking out the window.)* 'Tis her ladyship, sir. She always leaves her carriage in the next street. *(He starts to go off.)*

JOSEPH SURFACE. Wait. Let us draw the screen in front of the window. That old maid neighbor of mine is too curious for comfort. *(William and he draw the screen. William exits. Joseph crosses to the table right and looks at himself in the hand mirror.)* Well, I have a difficult hand to play now. I suspect Lady Teazle may have some notion as to my designs on Maria, but I mustn't let her into that little secret, at least not until I have her more in my power. *(Enter Lady Teazle from stage right.)*

LADY TEAZLE. Have you been very impatient? Oh Joseph, don't look so grave. I couldn't come before now.

JOSEPH SURFACE. Madam, punctuality is highly unfashionable

in a lady of quality.

LADY TEAZLE. *(Taking off her hat and gloves and putting them on the table, stage left.)* That may be, but I am an utter wreck! Sir Peter has grown so horrid to me and jealous of Charles, I am at my wit's end.

JOSEPH SURFACE. *(Aside, as he pours her a drink.)* I'm glad my friends are succeeding in that little endeavor.

LADY TEAZLE. *(Sitting in the wing chair.)* And now, Lady Sneerwell, who pretends to be my friend, has circulated scandalous tales about Charles and me.

JOSEPH SURFACE. *(Handing her the drink.)* It distresses me extremely to see you suffer such mortification.

LADY TEAZLE. Indeed, but for her to attack *me,* who never says ill of anybody ... that is, of any friend, at least. And to have Sir Peter so suspicious while I am innocent ...

JOSEPH SURFACE. My dear Lady, 'tis your own fault. *(Lady Teazle drinks.)*

LADY TEAZLE. Mine? How so?

JOSEPH SURFACE. When a husband groundlessly suspects his wife and withdraws his trust from her, she owes it to the honor of her sex to "outwit" him, shall we say?

LADY TEAZLE. Are you saying the best way to cure his jealousy is to give him reason for it?

JOSEPH SURFACE. Precisely. Husbands should never be deceived. 'Tis your very innocence that hurts you most and makes you victim of Sir Peter's outrageous accusations. Yes, my dear, your steadfast, unblemished, virtue.

LADY TEAZLE. You may very well be right.

JOSEPH SURFACE. Now, if you were to have a trifling little "affair," you would see how quickly the problem would vanish. Right now, you are absolutely dying from too much ... *purity.* If you follow my advice, all would be resolved in an instant.

LADY TEAZLE. So, I must sin in my own defense and part with my virtue in order to preserve my reputation?

JOSEPH SURFACE. You have it exactly. 'Tis *de rigueur* for a woman of fashion.

LADY TEAZLE. Well, this is certainly a most unique remedy for avoiding slander.

JOSEPH SURFACE. But an infallible one, trust me. *(He takes her hand and kneels by the side of the chair.)* And here, my precious, is the solution to all your problems.

LADY TEAZLE. If I could only be convinced it would be the proper …

JOSEPH SURFACE. *(Taking her handkerchief from her and smelling its perfume.)* Oh, certainly, you *should* be convinced. Of course. Heaven forbid I should persuade you to do anything you thought wrong. No, no, I have too much honor to desire it.

LADY TEAZLE. Don't you think we should leave honor out of the argument? If I am to be bedded by you, dear Joseph, it would be because of Sir Peter's vile behavior and not your *honorable* logic.

JOSEPH SURFACE. *(Embracing her.)* Whatever the reason, my dearest … *(Re-enter William from stage right.)*

WILLIAM. Sir…?

JOSEPH SURFACE. You blockhead, what do you want?

WILLIAM. Er … begging his pardon, sir, but I thought you would not choose Sir Peter to come up without announcing him.

JOSEPH SURFACE. Sir Peter? *Bloody hell!*

LADY TEAZLE. *(Running around the room.)* Sir Peter! Oh, God, I am ruined! *Ruined!*

WILLIAM. Sir, 'twas the maid who let him in. *(Joseph buttons his waist coat.)*

LADY TEAZLE. I'm completely demolished! What will become of me? *(The sound of Sir Peter coming up the stairs.)* Oh, my God, he's on the stairs! How could I ever have been so lunatic as to come here. *(She rushes Right.)*

JOSEPH SURFACE. The *screen! (She rushes behind the screen, leaving her handkerchief on the chair. To William.)* Hand me that book, you cretin! *(William hands him a book. Joseph sits down and pretends to be napping. William picks up a book and stands behind his chair, pretending to read. Enter Sir Peter Teazle with his walking stick.)*

SIR PETER TEAZLE. *(To William.)* Ay, ever improving himself, eh? *(William smiles and nods, then notices the book he is pretending to read is upside-down. He turns it over.)* Joseph? *(Sir Peter taps Joseph on the shoulder.)*

JOSEPH SURFACE. What? Oh, my dear Sir Peter, I humbly beg your pardon. *(Yawning. William yawns as well.)* I have been dozing over this stupid book. I am very pleased to see you. You haven't been here, I believe, since I fixed up this room. As you can see, books are my only vanity. *(William smiles and nods.)*

SIR PETER TEAZLE. Nay, nay, 'tis all very impressive. *(He goes to the screen and examines it.)* And I see you even make your screen a source of knowledge, as well; with all these maps.

JOSEPH SURFACE. Oh, yes, I find great use for that screen.

SIR PETER TEAZLE. I dare say. Handy when you want to find anything in a hurry, eh?

JOSEPH SURFACE. *(Aside.)* Ay, or to hide anything in a hurry. *(William has become deeply engrossed in the book.)*

SIR PETER TEAZLE. Joseph, I have a little private business ...

JOSEPH SURFACE. *(To William.)* You need not stay.

WILLIAM. I need not stay. No, sir. *(He does not move.)*

JOSEPH SURFACE. Get out!

WILLIAM. Get out. Yes, sir. *(He exits. As Sir Peter crosses stage right, Joseph rushes, picks up Lady Teazle's handkerchief from the chair where she left it, and quickly puts it in his pocket.)*

JOSEPH SURFACE. Here's a chair, Sir Peter. Sit, I beg you.

SIR PETER TEAZLE. Thank you. Now that we are alone, my boy, there is a subject that I wish to unburden to you. To be candid, Lady Teazle's conduct of late has made me terribly unhappy.

JOSEPH SURFACE. Oh, my friend, I am very sorry to hear it.

SIR PETER TEAZLE. 'Tis plain she has not the least regard for me.

JOSEPH SURFACE. I cannot believe that, Sir Peter!

SIR PETER TEAZLE. It's true. She has formed an attachment to someone else. And I think I've discovered who it is.

JOSEPH SURFACE. Sir Peter, you alarm me exceedingly. Such a discovery would hurt me just as much as you. *(Lady Teazle peeps out from behind the screen, unseen by Sir Peter. Joseph gestures for her to go back.)*

SIR PETER TEAZLE. Ah, Joseph, you have no idea what it means to me to have someone to whom I can trust my family secrets. But can't you guess who the knave is?

JOSEPH SURFACE. I haven't the most remote idea. Not Sir Benjamin Backbite?

SIR PETER TEAZLE. 'Tis *Charles*, your brother!

JOSEPH SURFACE. Impossible, sir! I cannot believe this of Lady Teazle. She has too much principle.

SIR PETER TEAZLE. What is principle against the flattery of a handsome, randy, young fellow?

JOSEPH SURFACE. *(Fluffing his neck lace.)* That's true, very true.

SIR PETER TEAZLE. If she were to commit an indiscretion and I were to make it public, the whole town would laugh at me and say I deserved it: a foolish, doddering, old bachelor who had married a child.

JOSEPH SURFACE. To be sure, they would laugh. *(Aside.)* Nay, *howl.* *(Aloud.)* Sir, if this be positively proven, then Charles is no longer a brother of mine. I irrevocably disclaim kinship with him. "For the man who can break the laws of hospitality, and tempt the wife of his friend, deserves to be branded as the foulest dreg of society."

SIR PETER TEAZLE. What noble sentiments! Ah, what a difference there is between you.

JOSEPH SURFACE. Still, I cannot believe you suspect Lady Teazle's honor.

SIR PETER TEAZLE. Joseph, I only wish to think well of her. She has lately reproached me more than once for having given her no financial means of her own. Therefore, I have decided she must be her own mistress with regard to money. *(He takes a document from his pocket.)* Here is a draft of my will I wish to have your opinion on. By it, she enjoys eight hundred a year independently while I live, and when I am carried to the great beyond, I most lovingly pass to her the bulk of my fortune."

JOSEPH SURFACE. *(Reading the will.)* Sir Peter, this bequest is astonishingly generous. *(Aside.)* Perhaps I should change horses.

SIR PETER TEAZLE. I am determined she shall have no cause to complain. But I would not have her know the proof of my love for her until this business with Charles is resolved.

JOSEPH SURFACE. *(Aside.)* Nor I, if I can help it.

SIR PETER TEAZLE. And now, dear friend, we will talk over the situation of your hopes with Maria.

JOSEPH SURFACE. *(Whispering.)* Oh, please, Sir Peter, another time. Your difficulties …

SIR PETER TEAZLE. I am saddened at the little progress you seem to make for her affections.

JOSEPH SURFACE. *(Whispering.)* I beg you will not mention it

SIR PETER TEAZLE. Eh? Speak up! What's happened to your voice?

JOSEPH SURFACE. *(Aside.)* 'Devil take him, I shall be *destroyed!*

SIR PETER TEAZLE. Listen to me, Joseph. Although you are averse to me telling Lady Teazle of your passion for Maria, I'm sure she's not your enemy in the affair.

JOSEPH SURFACE. *(Softly.)* Please, Sir Peter, oblige me. *Lady Teazle tries to escape and finds herself blocked by William. She scurries behind the screen as William re-enters from stage right.)* I am too overcome by your distresses to bestow a single thought on my own concerns.

WILLIAM. Sir…?

JOSEPH SURFACE. What now?

WILLIAM. Your brother has arrived and says he knows you are at home.

JOSEPH SURFACE. Tell him he is mistaken and that I'm out for the day.

SIR PETER TEAZLE. Wait, Joseph! A thought has struck me! You *shall* be at home, my good friend.

JOSEPH SURFACE. But he will interrupt us.

SIR PETER TEAZLE. I entreat you, please.

JOSEPH SURFACE. As you wish, Sir Peter. *(To William.)* Very well, show him up. *(Exit William.)*

SIR PETER TEAZLE. Here's what we will do. I will conceal myself somewhere, while you question him about Lady Teazle.

JOSEPH SURFACE. Oh, sir, would you have me join in so mean a trick on my dearest brother?

SIR PETER TEAZLE. If you are certain of his innocence, you do him the greatest service by giving him an opportunity to prove it. *(Moving to the door downstage left.)*

JOSEPH SURFACE. No, sir!

SIR PETER TEAZLE. *(Moving to the screen.)* I'll hide behind this screen then …

JOSEPH SURFACE. *(Grabbing him by the arm.)* No, Sir Peter! *(A flash of petticoat from behind the screen.)*

SIR PETER TEAZLE. What the devil! There seems to be someone here already! I'll swear I saw a petticoat!

JOSEPH SURFACE. *(Escorting him downstage, away from the screen.)* Ha, ha, ha! I know it's somewhat indiscreet of me, for though I hold a man of intrigue to be a most despicable character, I'm sure you agree it does not follow that one is to be an absolute saint, either. *(Whispering.)* 'Tis a little French dressmaker, a silly twit of a girl, who continually pursues me. Alarmed at losing some reputation on your coming, sir, she ran behind the screen.

SIR PETER TEAZLE. Oh, Joseph, Joseph, been naughty, have we? Well, 'tis only … But, egad, she has overheard all I have been saying about my wife!

JOSEPH SURFACE. Oh, 'twill never go any farther. I will swear her to secrecy.

SIR PETER TEAZLE. Are you certain?

JOSEPH SURFACE. On my honor, sir.

SIR PETER TEAZLE. Well then, I take you at your word. Let her hear it out. Where…?

JOSEPH SURFACE. The *closet!* Come quickly.

SIR PETER TEAZLE. *(Crossing to the closet stage right and closing the door.)* Sly, sly rogue!

JOSEPH SURFACE. Good God, I must keep my wits about me!

LADY TEAZLE. *(Starting out from behind the screen.)* Can I leave now?

JOSEPH SURFACE. *(Running to her and shooing her back behind the screen.)* No! Too dangerous, my dove!

SIR PETER TEAZLE. *(Peeping out of the closet.)* Joseph, remember, question him sharply.

JOSEPH SURFACE. *(Rushing back to the closet and closing the door.)* I will. Back, dear friend!

LADY TEAZLE. *(Peeping out from above the screen.)* Lock him in, lock him in! *(The sound of footsteps on the stairs.)*

JOSEPH SURFACE. *(Rushing to her and pushing her head down.)* I'm looking for the key, my *dearest!*

SIR PETER TEAZLE. *(Peeping out of the closet.)* Joseph, you're sure the little Frenchy won't blab?

JOSEPH SURFACE. *(Rushing back to the closet.)* On my life! In, *in,* my dear Sir Peter! *(He closes the door. Enter Charles Surface from stage right.)*

CHARLES SURFACE. What is going on here, brother? Your man would not let me up. Have you got a wench with you?

JOSEPH SURFACE. Ha, ha, ha, don't be ridiculous, Charles.

CHARLES SURFACE. I thought Sir Peter was here.

JOSEPH SURFACE. He was, but hearing you were coming, he chose not to stay.

CHARLES SURFACE. Still like that, is it?

JOSEPH SURFACE. I'm sorry to find you have lately given that worthy man grounds for great uneasiness.

CHARLES SURFACE. How so?

JOSEPH SURFACE. To be plain, he thinks you are trying to steal Lady Teazle's affections from him.

CHARLES SURFACE. Ha, ha, ha, ha! So the old codger has found he's got a young wife, has he? Or worse: that Lady Teazle has found she has an old husband?

JOSEPH SURFACE. This is no subject for jest, Charles.

CHARLES SURFACE. I never had the least inclination of what you charge me with, upon my honor.

JOSEPH SURFACE. *(Shouting.)* Well, I'm sure when Sir Peter hears that, it will be a great satisfaction to him!

CHARLES SURFACE. I am not yet *deaf,* brother. To be sure, I once thought the lady seemed to have taken a fancy to me, but I swear to you, I never gave her the least encouragement. Anyway, you know very well my attachment has always been to Maria.

JOSEPH SURFACE. But surely, if Lady Teazle had shown some affection for you ...

CHARLES SURFACE. Joseph, I hope I shall never deliberately commit a dishonorable action, but, well, if a pretty woman was purposely to throw herself at my feet, and that pretty woman was married to a man old enough to be her father, nay, her *grandfather* ... *(Sounds of protest from Sir Peter, in the closet.)*

JOSEPH SURFACE. Yes?

CHARLES SURFACE. Why, I believe I would ...

JOSEPH SURFACE. Yes?

CHARLES SURFACE. ... borrow a little of your morality, that's all. But you surprise me. I always understood *you* were Lady Teazle's favorite.

JOSEPH SURFACE. Oh, for shame, Charles! How can you say such a thing?

CHARLES SURFACE. Well, I've seen you exchange such significant glances. Don't deny it, now.

JOSEPH SURFACE. Nay, nay! Please do not say such things!

CHARLES SURFACE. I tell you I'm serious! Don't you remember one day, when I came here ...

JOSEPH SURFACE. Charles, *please...!*

CHARLES SURFACE. ... and found you two together.

JOSEPH SURFACE. Charles, I *insist! (Aside.)* My God, I must stop him!

CHARLES SURFACE. And yet another time, when your servant, William ...

JOSEPH SURFACE. *(Pulling him away from the closet.)* Be *still!* *(Pointing to the closet.)* Sir Peter has overheard all we have been saying. I knew you would clear yourself, or I should not have consented.

CHARLES SURFACE. What? Sir Peter, in there?

JOSEPH SURFACE. *(Whispering.) Yes!*

CHARLES SURFACE. By heaven, let's have him out. Sir Peter, come forth!

JOSEPH SURFACE. No, no...!

CHARLES SURFACE. Yes, yes! Sir Peter, come into court! *(Pulling Sir Peter out of the closet.)* What's this: my old guardian, turned inquisitor and gathering evidence incognito? Fie on you, sir!

SIR PETER TEAZLE. I most humbly beg your pardon, Charles,

but you mustn't be angry with Joseph. 'Twas all my idea. Please forgive me, my boy. I have suspected you wrongfully and you have completely acquitted yourself. What I have heard has chastened me and given me great satisfaction. And for that I heartily thank you, my dear, dear, Charles.

CHARLES SURFACE. Well, 'twas lucky you didn't hear any more, wasn't it, Joseph? You might have suspected my *dear, dear,* brother in this matter. *(Lady Teazle once more tries to sneak out, stage right, and once again William, entering, blocks her escape and forces her back behind the screen. William enters.)* Mightn't he, Joseph?

SIR PETER TEAZLE. Well, 'tis all done and I believe you. Come, embrace me, *(They embrace.)*

JOSEPH SURFACE. *(Aside.)* I must get them out of this *room!*

SIR PETER TEAZLE. And in future, perhaps, we may not be such strangers.

WILLIAM. *(Whispering to Joseph.)* Sir, Lady Sneerwell is below and says she will come up.

JOSEPH SURFACE. Lady Sneerwell? *(Whispering to William.)* *Imbecile!* You must stop her! Go! *(Exit William. Aside.)* I shall go mad! *(Trying to usher them out.)* Gentlemen, I beg pardon. I must wait on you downstairs. She has come on some business …

CHARLES SURFACE. Well, receive her elsewhere. Sir Peter and I have not seen each other for a long time, and I have something to say to him.

JOSEPH SURFACE. *(Aside.)* I cannot leave them together. *(Aloud.)* As you wish. I'll send Lady Sneerwell away, and return directly. *(Aside, to Sir Peter.)* Sir Peter, not a word of my French visitor.

SIR PETER TEAZLE. *(Aside, to Joseph.)* Oh, not for the world. *(Exit Joseph.)* Ah, Charles, if you associated more with your brother, one might indeed hope for your reformation. There is nothing in this universe so noble as a man of morals.

CHARLES SURFACE. Psha! He is so worried about his good name; he wouldn't let a priest *or* a wench into his house.

SIR PETER TEAZLE. Ha, ha, ha. No, no, you wrong him there, my boy. Joseph is no rake but then he is no saint either. *(Aside.)* I have a mind to tell him. Oh, we should have such a laugh.

CHARLES SURFACE. I just cannot abide all his puffed-up piety!

SIR PETER TEAZLE. No, no, you must not abuse him. *(Aside.)* I promised I wouldn't, but I'll tell him. *(Aloud.)* Charles, my dear, have you a mind to have a good laugh on Joseph?

CHARLES SURFACE. Oh, indeed, I should like it of all things.

SIR PETER TEAZLE. *(Whispering.)* You won't believe this, but he had a *girl* with him when I called.

CHARLES SURFACE. What? Joseph? Not in a hundred years!

SIR PETER TEAZLE. *(Whispering.)* Yes: a little French dressmaker! And best of all, she's still in the room now.

CHARLES SURFACE. The devil she is!

SIR PETER TEAZLE. She is, I tell you! Right there! *(He points to the screen.)*

CHARLES SURFACE. Behind the screen? Well, let's unveil her! *(The sound of footsteps on the stairs.)*

SIR PETER TEAZLE. No, no, you *mustn't!* He's coming back!

CHARLES SURFACE. Oh, the devil with him.

SIR PETER TEAZLE. Please, Charles, he will never forgive me!

CHARLES SURFACE. Blame me, then. Come out, my little bon-bon. Let's have a look at you.

SIR PETER TEAZLE. Egad, here he is!

CHARLES SURFACE. *(Looking behind the screen.)* Good God! *(Lady Teazle screams. The screen falls, exposing her. Re-enter Joseph Surface.)* Lady Teazle!

SIR PETER TEAZLE. *Lady Teazle,* by all that's damnable!

CHARLES SURFACE. Well, this is the most *stunning* French dressmaker I ever saw. Brother, will you please explain what has been going on here? *(Joseph is, for once, unable to respond except with a pitiful squeak.)* No? What, everyone mute? Right. Well, clearly this affair needs no further comment from me and since I see you three perfectly understand each other, I'll just leave you to it. *(Going.)* You were right, Sir Peter. There's nothing in this universe so noble as a man of virtue. *(He exits stage right, laughing.)*

JOSEPH SURFACE. Sir, I know appearances are against me, but if you will be patient, I shall explain everything to your satisfaction.

SIR PETER TEAZLE. If you please, sir.

JOSEPH SURFACE. Er, a ... the fact is, sir, that Lady Teazle, knowing my tender feelings for your ward, Maria.

LADY TEAZLE. What?

JOSEPH SURFACE. Rather, Lady Teazle, being distraught over your jealousy and temper ... and ... and ... knowing my friendship to the family ... she, sir, *yes* ... called here ... in order that ... *yes,* that I might explain things. *(His speech accelerating rapidly.)* Er ... but on your coming, being distraught, nay, fearful of your temper, she withdrew behind the screen. And this, on my honor, Sir Peter, is the complete and whole truth of the matter.

SIR PETER TEAZLE. A very clear account, sir. And I expect the lady will vouch for every detail.

LADY TEAZLE. Believe not a word, Sir Peter!

SIR PETER TEAZLE. What? You do not agree with these lies?

LADY TEAZLE. There is not one syllable of truth in what this *"gentleman"* has told you.

SIR PETER TEAZLE. I believe you, upon my soul I do, my dear.

JOSEPH SURFACE. *(Aside, to Lady Teazle.)* Madam, would you betray me?

LADY TEAZLE. Good Mr. Hypocrite, by your leave, I'll speak for myself.

SIR PETER TEAZLE. Oh, yes, let her alone. She'll concoct a much better story without any prompting from you.

LADY TEAZLE. Hear me, husband. I did not come here to speak of Maria. The truth is, I came, seduced by his insidious arguments, to listen to his pretended passion for me, and perhaps to sacrifice my honor and, I am ashamed to say, yours as well, to his treachery.

SIR PETER TEAZLE. Now I believe we are getting to the matter.

JOSEPH SURFACE. The woman's mad!

LADY TEAZLE. *(To Joseph.)* No, sir, she has recovered her senses, and your own devious arts have furnished her with the means! Sir Peter, I do not expect you to forgive me, but let me say the tenderness you expressed for me, not knowing I was a witness to it, has so penetrated to my heart that, had I left this place without the shame of your discovery, my future life and behavior would have spoken the sincerity of my gratitude. *(She is in tears. Joseph hands her her handkerchief.)* Thank you. *(She blows her nose.)* As for this smooth-tongued villain who would have seduced the wife of his too-credulous friend while plotting to steal his ward, I now see him in a light so utterly detestable, that I shall never again respect myself for ever having listened to him. *(She exits in tears.)*

JOSEPH SURFACE. She is mistaken! Sir Peter, heaven knows ...

SIR PETER TEAZLE. Be silent! Sir, you are a *villain!* I leave you to your conscience, if there is any of it left.

JOSEPH SURFACE. Sir Peter ... "The man who shuts out conviction by refusing to ... "

SIR PETER TEAZLE. Oh, to hell with your homilies! *(Calling after her.)* Lady Teazle, my dear, wait ... wait ... *(Exit Sir Peter stage right. Enter William from stage left.)*

WILLIAM. Mr. Stanley, sir.

JOSEPH SURFACE. *Stanley?* The plagues of Egypt on you, you

bumble-headed idiot! You *know* he comes to ask me for money.

WILLIAM. I wouldn't have let him in, sir, but Mr. Rowley came with him.

JOSEPH SURFACE. Rowley? Worse yet! Do I look as if I am in a state to receive visits from poor relations? Very well, very well, I suppose I am forced to see him if he's with Rowley. Show him up, nincompoop!

WILLIAM. Sir, 'tis not my fault Sir Peter found his lady …

JOSEPH SURFACE. Get out! *(Exit William.)* I am utterly *unbuttoned!* My reputation with Sir Peter, my hopes with Maria, destroyed in a moment! And now, curse me, I must listen to other people's problems! *(The sound of footsteps on the stairs.)* Here they come. I must have a moment to compose myself and put a little charity into my face. *(He exits stage left, to another room. Enter Sir Oliver Surface and Rowley from stage right. Sir Oliver wears a tattered coat and hat.)*

SIR OLIVER SURFACE. What? Does he avoid us? That was he, was it not?

ROWLEY. It was, sir, but I believe his nerves are so weak, the sight of a destitute relative may be too much for him. I should have gone first to break it to him.

SIR OLIVER SURFACE. A plague on his nerves! And this the man whom Sir Peter extols as a man of benevolence?

ROWLEY. I'll depart until you finish and leave, then come back and announce your arrival as your true self.

SIR OLIVER SURFACE. And meet me afterwards at Sir Peter's.

ROWLEY. Without losing a moment. *(He exits stage right.)*

SIR OLIVER SURFACE. I like not the look of this "philanthropic" smile that approaches. *(Re-enter Joseph Surface from stage left, wearing his coat.)*

JOSEPH SURFACE. Ah, sir, I beg your pardon for keeping you waiting. Mr. Stanley, I presume?

SIR OLIVER SURFACE. *(Bowing.)* At your service.

JOSEPH SURFACE. I pray you will do me the honor to sit down, nay, I entreat you, sir.

SIR OLIVER SURFACE. Thank you. *(Aside.)* A bit *too* civil, if you ask me.

JOSEPH SURFACE. Mr. Stanley, I am so happy to see you. You were nearly related to my mother, I think?

SIR OLIVER SURFACE. I was, sir, so nearly that my present poverty, I am sorry to say, forces me to trouble her wealthy children; otherwise I should not have presumed to come.

JOSEPH SURFACE. *(Pouring a drink.)* Oh, dear sir, there needs be no apology. "He that is in distress, though a stranger, has a right to claim kindred with the wealthy." *(Sir Oliver, thinking the drink is for him, reaches for it, but Joseph drains the glass.)* Alas, I only wish I was one of that class and had it in my power to offer you even a small relief.

SIR OLIVER SURFACE. You cannot help me, then? *(Joseph shakes his head.)* Ah, if only your uncle, Sir Oliver, were here, I might have sought assistance from him.

JOSEPH SURFACE. My dear Stanley, I doubt if you could expect anything from him. He is a wealthy man, a very wealthy man, but avarice, sir, is the vice of old age. I will tell you in confidence he has done nothing for me, though people, I know, think otherwise ...

SIR OLIVER SURFACE. What? Has he never sent you bullion, rupees, letters of credit?

JOSEPH SURFACE. *(Laughs.)* Oh, dear sir, nothing of the kind! No, no, a few trifling presents now and then: a bit of tea, crackers, a few jars of Indian pickle.

SIR OLIVER SURFACE. *(Aside.)* Crackers and *pickle?* Here's gratitude for twelve thousand pounds!

JOSEPH SURFACE. And then, I am sad to say, there is the dreadful extravagance of my brother. Oh, Mr. Stanley, the sums I have lent him! Well, perhaps I am to blame. It's a weakness in me. And now I feel doubly at fault, since it has deprived me of the pleasure of helping you, poor sir, as my heart would desire.

SIR OLIVER SURFACE. *(Aside.)* Oh, the knave! *(To Joseph.)* Then there is absolutely no hope of help from you?

JOSEPH SURFACE. For the present, it grieves me to say *no,* but whenever I have the ability, you may depend upon hearing from me.

SIR OLIVER SURFACE. I am desolated, Mr. Surface.

JOSEPH SURFACE. Not more than I, believe me. "To pity, without the power to relieve, is more painful than to ask and be denied."

SIR OLIVER SURFACE. Kind sir, your most obedient, humble, servant.

JOSEPH SURFACE. *(Feigning tears.)* Oh, dear, you leave me deeply affected, Mr. Stanley. *(Shouting.)* William, be ready to open the door!

SIR OLIVER SURFACE. Oh, please, no ceremony. *(He starts out. Joseph moves downstage, thinking Sir Oliver is going. Sir Oliver stops and bows.)* Your most obsequious.

JOSEPH SURFACE. *(Joseph moves back upstage, to him, and makes leg and flourish .)* You may depend upon hearing from me, whenever I can be of service. *(Sir Oliver moves further upstage. Joseph moves*

downstage, thinking he is gone. Sir Oliver stops and bows again.)
SIR OLIVER SURFACE. You are too good.
JOSEPH SURFACE. *(Joseph moves to him once again, bows, makes leg and flourish, this time more elaborately. Sir Oliver starts to leave once more.* In the meantime, I wish you health and good spirits. *(Once again Joseph moves downstage.)*
SIR OLIVER SURFACE. Your ever grateful and humble servant. *(The sound of footsteps on the stairs.)*
JOSEPH SURFACE. *(Exasperated now, Joseph returns upstage and makes his most elaborate and exaggerated bow, leg, and flourish.)* Sir, yours as sincerely.
SIR OLIVER SURFACE. *(Aside.)* Now I am satisfied. *(He exits stage right.)*
JOSEPH SURFACE. *(Sinking into a chair.)* Egad! The appalling thing about having good character is that it always invites desperate appeals from poor relatives and requires an exhausting amount of effort to establish a reputation of benevolence without incurring the expense. *(Enter Rowley from stage right.)*
ROWLEY. Mr. Surface, your servant. Excuse me, but my business demands immediate attention, as this note will inform you. *(He hands him a note.)*
JOSEPH SURFACE. Nay, nay, always happy to see you, Mr. Rowley, *(Aside, as he reads the note.)* Rascal though you are. What's this? Sir Oliver has arrived?
ROWLEY. Indeed, sir. We have just parted. He is quite well and eager to embrace his worthy nephew.
JOSEPH SURFACE. I am utterly astonished, Rowley!
ROWLEY. I came only to tell you and now I must be gone to inform your brother and direct him here to meet your uncle who will be with you shortly.
JOSEPH SURFACE. *(Aside.)* Never was anything so damned unlucky!
ROWLEY. You will be delighted to see how well he looks.
JOSEPH SURFACE. I'm utterly *overwhelmed* ... *(Aside.)* Just at the wrong time!
ROWLEY. I'll tell him how impatiently you expect him.
JOSEPH SURFACE. Do, do! Pray give him my best duty and affection. I cannot *express* the sensations I feel at the thought of seeing him. *(Exit Rowley, stage right.)* The devil take it! His coming just now is the cruelest piece of ill-fortune. Yaaaah, I shall completely lose my mind! *(Joseph exits stage left.)*

Scene 2

Sir Peter Teazle's parlor — early evening. The furniture is as seen previously, except that most of the flowers have been removed. Enter Mrs. Candor and Maid from stage right.

MAID. Ma'am, Lady Teazle will see no one at present.

MRS. CANDOR. Did you tell her it was her friend, Mrs. Candor?

MAID. Yes, ma'am, but she begs you will excuse her.

MRS. CANDOR. Go again and tell her I want to see her only for a moment. I'm sure she must be in great distress, dear heart. *(Exit Maid. Mrs. Candor moves to the table, pours herself a glass of Sir Peter's rare brandy, and drinks it down.)* How frustrating, not to know all the details! The whole affair will be in the newspapers, with the names of all the parties, before I have told the story at a dozen houses. *(Enter Sir Benjamin Backbite.)* Oh, dear Sir Benjamin, you've heard, I suppose …

SIR BENJAMIN BACKBITE. Of Lady Teazle and Joseph?

MRS. CANDOR. Of Sir Peter's discovery.

SIR BENJAMIN BACKBITE. Oh, the most tawdry piece of business, to be sure!

MRS. CANDOR. Well, I never was so surprised in my life. I am sorry for the parties, indeed,

SIR BENJAMIN BACKBITE. *(Helping himself to the brandy.)* I confess I don't pity Sir Peter at all. He was too extravagantly partial to Joseph.

MRS. CANDOR. Joseph? Why, 'twas with Charles Lady Teazle was found!

SIR BENJAMIN BACKBITE. No, no, I tell you. *Joseph* is the cad!

MRS. CANDOR. No such thing! 'Twas *Charles!* Joseph brought Sir Peter on purpose to discover them.

SIR BENJAMIN BACKBITE. I tell you I had it from one …

MRS. CANDOR. And *I* have it from one …

SIR BENJAMIN BACKBITE. Who had it from one, who had it …

MRS. CANDOR. From the *other one*, directly! But here comes Lady Sneerwell. Perhaps she knows about it. *(She pours herself another brandy and drinks. Enter Lady Sneerwell from stage right.)*

LADY SNEERWELL. Ah, my dear Mrs. Candor, here's a sad affair!

MRS. CANDOR. Indeed. Who would have thought ...

LADY SNEERWELL. *(Pouring herself a brandy and drinking.)* Well, there is no trusting to appearances, though Lady Teazle *was* always a bit too lively for me.

MRS. CANDOR. I agree. Her manners are a little too free, but then she is so young.

LADY SNEERWELL. And yet has a *few* good qualities.

MRS. CANDOR. So she has. Have you heard all the particulars?

LADY SNEERWELL. No, but everybody says that Joseph ...

SIR BENJAMIN BACKBITE. There, I told you it was Joseph!

MRS. CANDOR. No, no! Charles was the seducer!

LADY SNEERWELL. *Charles?* You alarm me, Mrs. Candor! Are you sure?

MRS. CANDOR. Yes, yes. *He* was the lover. Joseph was only the informer.

SIR BENJAMIN BACKBITE. Well. I only hope that Sir Peter's wound will not ...

MRS. CANDOR. *Wound?* Oh, dear God, I didn't hear a word of any fighting!

LADY SNEERWELL. Nor I; not a syllable.

SIR BENJAMIN BACKBITE. What, no mention of the duel?

MRS. CANDOR. Nothing.

SIR BENJAMIN BACKBITE. Oh, yes, they fought before they left the room.

LADY SNEERWELL. Pray let us hear the details.

MRS. CANDOR. Yes, please.

SIR BENJAMIN BACKBITE. "Sir," says Sir Peter, immediately after the discovery, "you are a most ungrateful cad."

MRS. CANDOR. To Charles.

SIR BENJAMIN BACKBITE. No, no, to *Joseph!* "You are a most ungrateful cad and, old as I am, sir," says he, "I insist on immediate satisfaction!"

MRS. CANDOR. That *must* have been to Charles, for 'tis very unlikely Joseph would fight in his own house.

SIR BENJAMIN BACKBITE. Gad's life, madam, *no!* " ... immediate satisfaction!" says Sir Peter. On this, Lady Teazle, seeing Sir Peter in grave danger, ran out of the room in howling hysterics, with Charles after her. Then madam, Sir Peter and Joseph began to fight with swords. *(Enter Crabtree from stage right.)*

CRABTREE. With pistols, nephew, *pistols!* I have it from an unimpeachable authority.

MRS. CANDOR. Oh, Mr. Crabtree, then it is all true!

CRABTREE. *(Pouring himself a brandy and drinking.)* Too true, indeed, madam, and Sir Peter is critically wounded.

SIR BENJAMIN BACKBITE. By a thrust through his left side.

CRABTREE. By a bullet to the thorax!

MRS. CANDOR. Mercy! Poor Sir Peter!

CRABTREE. Indeed, madam. Charles would have avoided the duel, if he could, but …

MRS. CANDOR. *(To Backbite.)* There, you see? It *was* Charles!

SIR BENJAMIN BACKBITE. My uncle knows nothing of the matter.

CRABTREE. … Sir Peter accused him of the basest ingratitude …

SIR BENJAMIN BACKBITE. *I* told you that!

CRABTREE. Do, nephew, let me speak! … and insisted on immediate satisfaction.

SIR BENJAMIN BACKBITE. Just as I said.

CRABTREE. Egad, nephew, allow others to know something, will you? A pair of loaded pistols lay on the bureau.

SIR BENJAMIN BACKBITE. Pistols? I heard nothing of this.

CRABTREE. *(Enacting the scene.)* Sir Peter forced Charles to take one. They fired simultaneously. Charles's shot found its mark, as I told you, but Sir Peter's missed. *(Suddenly puzzled.)* But what is quite extraordinary … *(His finger tracing the trajectory, Mrs. Candor's, Lady Sneerwell's, and Sir Benjamin's head, following Crabtree's finger.)* … the bullet struck against a little bronze Shakespeare that stood over the fireplace, glanced at a right angle across the room to a bust of Voltaire on the desk, then ricocheted back out the window and struck the postman, in the head, who was just coming to the door with a letter from Liverpool, postage due in the amount of tuppence and a ha' penny.

MRS. CANDOR. *(Pouring herself a brandy and drinking.)* How very odd.

SIR BENJAMIN BACKBITE. My uncle's account may be more circumstantial but mine is the true one, whatever he says.

LADY SNEERWELL. *(Aside.)* I must have better information. *(She exits.)*

SIR BENJAMIN BACKBITE. Ah, Lady Sneerwell's alarm is easily accounted for.

CRABTREE. Yes, yes, they all say she and Charles ... But that's for another time.

MRS. CANDOR. *(Now somewhat fuzzy.)* Where is Sir Peter at present?

CRABTREE. *(Pouring himself a brandy and drinking. The bottle is now empty.)* Oh, they brought him home and he is now here in the house, though the servants are ordered to deny all visitors.

MRS. CANDOR. And Lady Teazle, I suppose, is attending him?

CRABTREE. Yes, of course.

SIR BENJAMIN BACKBITE. But who comes here?

CRABTREE. It must be the physician.

MRS. CANDOR. Oh, finally. The physician. Now we shall know everything. *(Enter Sir Oliver from stage left.)*

CRABTREE. Doctor, can you offer any hope?

MRS. CANDOR. Yes, doctor, is he near the end?

SIR BENJAMIN BACKBITE. Doctor, is it not a wound with a small sword?

CRABTREE. I tell you, a bullet lodged in the thorax!

SIR OLIVER SURFACE. *Doctor?* A wound with a small sword and a bullet in the thorax? Egad, are you all mad?

SIR BENJAMIN BACKBITE. Perhaps, sir, you are not a doctor?

SIR OLIVER SURFACE. I thank you for my degree, if I am.

CRABTREE. Ah, a friend of Sir Peter's then, I presume. But, sir, you must have heard of his duel?

SIR OLIVER SURFACE. I have not.

CRABTREE. Nor of his being dangerously wounded?

SIR OLIVER SURFACE. The devil he is!

SIR BENJAMIN BACKBITE. Run through the body.

CRABTREE. Shot in the breast.

SIR BENJAMIN BACKBITE. By Joseph Surface!

CRABTREE. *Charles!*

MRS. CANDOR. Yes *Charles!* On the other hand, it could have been Joseph.

SIR OLIVER SURFACE. All of you seem to differ strangely in your accounts. However, you agree that Sir Peter is dangerously wounded?

SIR BENJAMIN BACKBITE. Oh, yes, we agree in that.

CRABTREE. Yes, yes, there is no doubt of it.

SIR OLIVER SURFACE. Well, for a person in his condition, he is the most reckless man alive, for here he comes, walking as if nothing at all was the matter. *(Sir Peter enters from stage left.)* Sir

Peter, you have come in good time. We are about to hold your funeral and bury you!

SIR BENJAMIN BACKBITE. *(Aside to Crabtree.)* Egad, uncle, this is a most sudden recovery!

SIR OLIVER SURFACE. *(To Sir Peter.)* My dear man, what are you doing out of bed with a sword through your body and a bullet in your thorax?

SIR PETER TEAZLE. A sword and a bullet? What the devil is all this?

SIR BENJAMIN BACKBITE. Sir Peter, we rejoice that the story of the duel is not true, but are sincerely sorry for your other misfortune.

SIR PETER TEAZLE. *(Aside.)* All over the town already.

CRABTREE. Though, you must admit you are to blame for marrying at your age.

SIR PETER TEAZLE. What business is that of yours, sir?

MRS. CANDOR. Now then, we must admit Sir Peter made a good husband and is very much to be pitied.

SIR PETER TEAZLE. Plague on your pity, ma'am. I desire none of it!

SIR BENJAMIN BACKBITE. *(To Sir Peter.)* Poor man, you must try to ignore the laughter and jeers you are bound to meet with from now on.

CRABTREE. 'Tis is a common occurrence. That's one comfort.

SIR PETER TEAZLE. I insist on all of you leaving my house *immediately!*

MRS. CANDOR. Yes, let us all go. And you may rest assured, Sir Peter, we'll make the best report of the whole sordid affair that we can. *(She pinches his cheek and exits laughing and staggering.)*

CRABTREE. Indeed! And explain to everyone how badly you've been treated.

SIR PETER TEAZLE. Out! *(Crabtree starts to leave.)*

SIR BENJAMIN BACKBITE. And how patiently you bear it. *(He crosses stage right, following Crabtree.)*

SIR PETER TEAZLE. *(Chasing them.)* Fiends! Vipers! Furies! *(He reaches for his brandy and finds the bottle empty.)* Oh, that their own venom would choke them!

SIR OLIVER SURFACE. Amen to that, Sir Peter. *(Enter Rowley from stage right.)*

ROWLEY. I heard argumentation. Is something amiss, sir?

SIR PETER TEAZLE. When is it not? Do I ever pass a day without tortures and vexations?

ROWLEY. Er ... perhaps this is not a good time to ask the question ...

SIR OLIVER SURFACE. *(To Sir Peter.)* Well, my friend, I have tested both my nephews in the manner we proposed. Joseph is indeed the man for Maria, after all.

ROWLEY. He is, as you say, " ... a man of principles." 'Tis pure edification to hear him speak.

SIR OLIVER SURFACE. A splendid model for the young men of the age! But what's this, my friend? You don't join us in adulation?

SIR PETER TEAZLE. I do not! We live in a damned wicked world and the fewer we praise the better, and least of all Joseph Surface. I see by your grinning you have heard of the whole affair.

ROWLEY. I am indeed acquainted with the sad events, good sir. I met Lady Teazle coming from Joseph's house so humbled, she pleaded with me to be her advocate with you.

SIR PETER TEAZLE. *(To Sir Oliver.)* You know about all of this, as well?

SIR OLIVER SURFACE. Every circumstance.

SIR PETER TEAZLE. About the closet and the screen?

SIR OLIVER SURFACE. Yes, yes, and the little French bon-bon. I have been vastly amused by the story! Ha, ha, ha!

SIR PETER TEAZLE. Yes, very entertaining.

SIR OLIVER SURFACE. I never laughed more in my life. Ha, ha, ha!

SIR PETER TEAZLE. Uncommonly hilarious. Ha, ha, ha!

ROWLEY. Joseph and his morality! Ha, ha, ha!

SIR PETER TEAZLE. Ha, ha, ha! Hypocritical villain!

SIR OLIVER SURFACE. Ay, and that rascal, Charles, to pull you out of the closet. Ha, ha, ha!

SIR PETER TEAZLE. Ha, ha! A great comedy!

SIR OLIVER SURFACE. Ha, ha, ha! I would like to have seen your expression when the screen came crashing down. Ha, ha!

SIR PETER TEAZLE. Yes, my expression when the screen crashed down. Ha, ha, ha! Oh, I can never show my face again!

SIR OLIVER SURFACE. Oh. but come, come, it isn't fair to laugh at you, my old friend, though, upon my soul, I can't help it.

SIR PETER TEAZLE. Oh, pray don't restrain yourselves on my account. Being a standing joke for all one's friends is very comical.

ROWLEY. Sir Peter, Lady Teazle is there, in the hall. I am sure you must desire reconciliation as much as she does.

SIR OLIVER SURFACE. Perhaps my being here prevents her coming to you. I'll leave Rowley to mediate between you, but he must bring you all to Joseph's house, where I will return presently as my authentic self, to expose more hypocrisy.

SIR PETER TEAZLE. Oh, rest assured. I will be there. *(Sir Oliver exits stage right.)* She's not coming in here, Rowley. She's gone into the next room.

ROWLEY. But has left the door open on purpose, as you can see. Oh, dear, she is in tears.

SIR PETER TEAZLE. So she is. A little mortification is very becoming in a wife, don't you think? It will do her good to let her lament her sins a little.

ROWLEY. Sir Peter, forgive me, but this is ungenerous in you, sir.

SIR PETER TEAZLE. I am at my wit's end, Rowley! I know not what to think. I cannot put those letters of hers to Charles out of my mind.

ROWLEY. I told you, they are forgeries, sir. Of that I am certain.

SIR PETER TEAZLE. If I could only be sure. Look, Rowley, look at her. What a remarkably elegant turn of the head she has.

ROWLEY. Go to her and comfort her, my lord.

SIR PETER TEAZLE. I will. I cannot do otherwise, I love her so. Though, heaven help me, when it is known we have made up, people will laugh at me ten times more.

ROWLEY. Let them, and answer their malice by showing them you are happy in spite of it.

SIR PETER TEAZLE. By God, I will try Rowley, while there is still a chance for us. We may yet be happy.

ROWLEY. Remember, sir, "He who once lays aside suspicion ... "

SIR PETER TEAZLE. *Cease!* If you have any regard for me, Rowley, never let me hear you utter that excrement again. I have had enough virtuous sentiments to serve me the rest of my life. *(Sir Peter exits stage left. Rowley exits stage right.)*

Scene 3

Library in Joseph Surface's house — as seen previously. A short time later. Enter Joseph Surface and Lady Sneerwell from stage right.

LADY SNEERWELL. Sir Peter instantly reconciled to Charles and no longer opposes his marriage to Maria? *Impossible!* Just the thought of it makes me ill.

JOSEPH SURFACE. Can your passion furnish a remedy?

LADY SNEERWELL. No, nor cunning either. I was a fool, an idiot, to join with such a blunderer!

JOSEPH SURFACE. Lady Sneerwell, I suffer the *deepest* wound, but as you see, bear the pain with calmness.

LADY SNEERWELL. Of course, your interest is only for Maria's fortune. The disappointment doesn't touch your *heart*. If you really felt for her what I feel for Charles, neither your temper nor your hypocrisy could prevent you showing the depths of your despair.

JOSEPH SURFACE. But why do you reproach me for your disappointment?

LADY SNEERWELL. Because you are the cause of it! It wasn't enough for you to deceive Sir Peter about Charles and win Maria, but you had to seduce his wife as well. *(Aside, to the audience.)* I hate such greed in crime, don't you? 'Tis an unfair monopoly.

JOSEPH SURFACE. Well, I admit I did deviate from my purpose a bit, but I don't think we're totally defeated yet. Do you believe Snake is still faithful to us?

LADY SNEERWELL. I do.

JOSEPH SURFACE. And will he swear by those letters he forged that Charles has contracted himself by vows of love to you?

LADY SNEERWELL. Of course he will.

JOSEPH SURFACE. Well, then, we still may have one last chance of rescuing the situation. *(Knocking at the door.)* Ah, this is probably my uncle, Sir Oliver. Retire to the next room and we'll talk more when he's gone.

LADY SNEERWELL. What if Sir Peter tells him of your deceptions?

JOSEPH SURFACE. Oh, I have no fear of that. He will hold his tongue to protect his reputation *and* Lady Teazle's. You may count on it. And with a little finesse, I will soon discover Sir Oliver's vulnerabilities.

LADY SNEERWELL. I am confident in your skills, Joseph, but only one roguery at a time, if you please.

JOSEPH SURFACE. Yes, yes, I promise you. *(Pointing to door left.)* In there! Go! *(Exit Lady Sneerwell through the door downstage left.)* 'Tis damned vexing to be harangued by one's accomplice in evil. *(He looks offstage right.)* What's this, old Stanley again? Devil take him! If Sir Oliver finds him here and they speak, I am undone beyond redemption. *(Enter Oliver Surface from stage right.)* On my life, Mr. Stanley, why have you come back to plague me at this time? I thought we had concluded ... William? *William!*

SIR OLIVER SURFACE. Oh, sir, splendid news! I have just heard your uncle Oliver is expected here momentarily, and even though he has been not as generous to you as you would like, he may yet do something for me.

JOSEPH SURFACE. No! 'Tis impossible for you to stay right now. Come any other time, and I promise you ...

SIR OLIVER SURFACE. But if Sir Oliver could only be acquainted with my situation ... *(The sound of footsteps on the stairs.)*

JOSEPH SURFACE. Zounds, sir, I insist on you *leaving immediately!*

SIR OLIVER SURFACE. Nay. There may be a chance ...

JOSEPH SURFACE. I want you out! Now! William, show this leech out! *William!* Curse him! I will not tolerate such insolence! *(He puts his arm around Sir Oliver's neck and tries to drag him out, choking him. Enter Charles from stage right.)*

CHARLES SURFACE. Hold there, Joseph! What the devil are you doing to my friend? *Brother,* take your hands off him, I say! *(To Sir Oliver.)* Are you all right, my dear fellow? *(Sir Oliver holds his throat, gasping for breath, unable to speak.)*

JOSEPH SURFACE. So, he's been to see you as well, has he?

CHARLES SURFACE. To be sure he has. Why, he's as honest a ... Joseph, you haven't been asking him for money too, have you?

JOSEPH SURFACE. Of course not! Have you forgotten we expect Sir Oliver here any...?

CHARLES SURFACE. Gadzooks, you're right! Old Ollie mustn't find I've been borrowing.

JOSEPH SURFACE. But this Stanley refuses to ...

CHARLES SURFACE. Stanley? His name is Farquhar.

JOSEPH SURFACE. I tell you it is *Stanley!*

CHARLES SURFACE. It's *Farquhar!*

JOSEPH SURFACE. I don't care *what* he calls himself! He must leave now! *(Knocking below.) Devils and damnation,* Sir Oliver is at the door! Mr. Stanley, you must get out of here. Do you hear me?

CHARLES SURFACE. Yes, yes! Please vacate, Mr. Farquhar …

SIR OLIVER SURFACE. *(Finally able to speak.)* Gentlemen, I will not!

JOSEPH SURFACE. *(Grabbing him again and trying to pull him off.)* You meddling old fool, by heaven, you *shall* go!

CHARLES SURFACE. *(Assisting Joseph.)* Yes, out with him, quickly! *(The sound of footsteps on the stairs.)*

SIR OLIVER SURFACE. Unhand me, you villains! Help! This is violence…! *Help!*

CHARLES SURFACE. *(They pick him up and start to carry him off, stage left.)* Out with him! Out, out, out! *(Enter William from stage right.)*

WILLIAM. Sir Peter, Lady Teazle, and … *(Charles and Joseph stumble, and drop Sir Oliver, and fall on top of him in a heap. Sir Oliver once more loses his wig in the scuffle. Enter Sir Peter, Lady Teazle, Rowley, and Maria from stage right. Rowley carries Sir Oliver's coat.)*

SIR PETER TEAZLE. *Great Caesar's ghost!* What mischief is here; nephews assaulting their uncle on the day of his arrival? Sir Oliver…? *(Joseph and Charles, shocked, drift downstage right, to the table.)*

LADY TEAZLE. Oh, Sir Oliver, 'twas well we came to rescue you.

ROWLEY. *(Retrieving Sir Oliver's wig and putting it on his head, then helping him to take off his tattered coat and put on the one he has brought for him.)* Indeed, for I see the character of poor Stanley was no protection. *(William slinks offstage.)*

SIR OLIVER SURFACE. *(Collecting himself.)* Nor of Farquhar either. The needs of the former could not extract a shilling from that "benevolent" gentleman. *(Pointing to Joseph.)* And with Charles, I stood a chance of being sold with my ancestors!

JOSEPH SURFACE. *Charles?*

CHARLES SURFACE. *Joseph?*

JOSEPH SURFACE. *(Sinking into a chair.)* 'Tis now complete!

CHARLES SURFACE. *(Sinking into a chair.)* Disastrously concluded.

SIR OLIVER SURFACE. *(Pointing again at Joseph.)* Behold this knave! You well know what he has received from my bounty and how gladly I would have given half my fortune to be held in trust for him. Imagine my disappointment in discovering him to be destitute of truth, charity, *and* gratitude!

SIR PETER TEAZLE. Sir Oliver, I should be shocked at your opinion had I not myself found him to be mean, treacherous, and hypocritical.

LADY TEAZLE. And if the gentleman pleads not guilty to these charges, pray let me give references as to his character.

SIR PETER TEAZLE. My dear, I believe we need add no more. The most perfect punishment is that he is now known to the entire world.

CHARLES SURFACE. *(Aside.)* Egad, if they talk this way about virtue, what will they say of me? *(Sir Peter, Lady Teazle, and Maria converse.)*

SIR OLIVER SURFACE. As for his prodigal brother, there …

CHARLES SURFACE. *(Aside.)* Ay, my turn. The damned family pictures have sunk me!

JOSEPH SURFACE. Sir Oliver, dear uncle, will you let me explain?

CHARLES SURFACE. *(Aside.)* Yes, *please*, Joseph, make one of your long speeches on morality. It may give me time to think of a defense.

SIR OLIVER SURFACE. *(To Joseph.)* You think you could justify yourself, sir?

JOSEPH SURFACE. I am confident I could, uncle.

SIR OLIVER SURFACE. *(To Charles.)* And *you*, sir, could justify yourself with an explanation as well, I suppose?

CHARLES SURFACE. Ah … not just yet, but I am presently endeavoring to contrive one.

SIR OLIVER SURFACE. Scoundrel!

ROWLEY. Come, Sir Oliver, I know you cannot speak of Charles's follies with anger.

SIR OLIVER SURFACE. Nay, on my heart, I cannot, nor with any gravity either.

CHARLES SURFACE. Sir Oliver, believe me sincere when I tell you if I do not appear humiliated at the exposure of my crimes it is because at this moment I feel the deepest and warmest satisfaction at seeing you here, my dearest uncle and most liberal benefactor.

SIR OLIVER SURFACE. Well, I believe you Charles, and will make my peace with you. *(Holding out his arms.)* Embrace me, nephew. *(They embrace.)*

CHARLES SURFACE. Sir, my gratitude for your forgiveness is without limit.

LADY TEAZLE. Yet, I believe, Sir Oliver, there is someone here, as well, to whom Charles, I think, is still more anxious to be reconciled. *(She turns to Maria.)*

SIR OLIVER SURFACE. Oh, I have heard of his attachment there and with the young lady's pardon, if I construe right, I see a little blush...?

SIR PETER TEAZLE. Well, child, speak your heart.

MARIA. *(To Sir Oliver.)* Sir, I have little to say but that I rejoice you and Charles are reunited and happy. But for me, whatever claim I had to his feelings, I willingly surrender to one who seems to have a better right to them.

CHARLES SURFACE. What are you talking about, Maria?

SIR PETER TEAZLE. What's this? While he appeared an incorrigible rake, you would give your hand to no one else and now that he is likely to reform, you won't have him?

MARIA. His own heart and Lady Sneerwell know the cause.

CHARLES SURFACE. *Lady Sneerwell?*

JOSEPH SURFACE. Brother, though it pains me deeply, in the cause of justice, I am compelled to speak. Lady Sneerwell's injuries and broken heart can no longer be concealed. *(He crosses downstage left and opens the door.)* Enter, my poor woman. *(Enter Lady Sneerwell, with a pillow stuffed under her gown to make her appear pregnant.)*

SIR OLIVER SURFACE. What, another French dressmaker? Egad, he's got one in every room in the house!

CHARLES SURFACE. Lady Sneerwell?

LADY SNEERWELL. Ungrateful, Charles! *(Indicating her abdominal protrusion.)* Oh, well may you be surprised to see exposed the condition your perfidy has forced me into.

CHARLES SURFACE. Uncle, is this another plot of yours? On my life, I am completely confounded by these accusations.

JOSEPH SURFACE. I believe, sir, there is the evidence of but one more person necessary to make things unmistakably clear.

SIR PETER TEAZLE. Indeed. And you will, of course, say that person is Mr. Snake. Pray let him appear, Rowley.

ROWLEY. Mr. Snake, walk in. *(Snake enters.)* We anticipated his testimony might be wanted. But, as it happens, unfortunately for her, he comes to confront Lady Sneerwell, not to support her.

LADY SNEERWELL. *(To Snake.)* Judas! Have you betrayed me?

SNAKE. *(Bowing.)* I beg your ladyship ten thousand and one pardons. *(Taking out letters.)* You paid me extremely well to forge these letters between Charles and Lady Teazle and the one of his marriage contract to you, as well. *(He turns to Rowley and hands him the letters.)* But this generous gentleman gave me double the amount to speak the truth.

LADY SNEERWELL. *(Going.)* May you rot in hell, Snake! And the torments of shame and disappointment on the rest of you!

LADY TEAZLE. Wait, *dear* lady. Before you go, I wish you to inform that scandalous college, of which you are illustrious president without peer, that Lady Teazle, former graduate, returns the diploma they granted her, leaves off the practice of slander, and promises to kill character no longer.

LADY SNEERWELL. A pox on you, you insolent cur! *(She exits stage right.)*

SIR PETER TEAZLE. Egad, what fury!

LADY TEAZLE. Despicable creature!

SIR OLIVER SURFACE. *(To Joseph.)* Well, sir, and what have you to say now?

JOSEPH SURFACE. Uncle, I am utterly horrified to find Lady Sneerwell could be guilty of using Mr. Snake in this manner, and to prevent her revengeful spirit from injuring my brother any further, I had better follow her to foil any more of her dreadful machinations. *(Joseph exits stage right.)*

SIR PETER TEAZLE. Moral to the last!

SIR OLIVER SURFACE. *(Calling after Joseph.)* Why don't you marry *her,* Joseph? Oil and vinegar! By heaven, you'll go very well together.

ROWLEY. *(Indicating Snake.)* I believe we have no more need for this "person."

SNAKE. Dear Sirs and Ladies, before I go I beg pardon for whatever unpleasantness I have caused to all the parties present.

SIR PETER TEAZLE. Well, you have made atonement by one good deed at least.

SNAKE. Oh, *please,* I must beg all of you that my part in this affair be kept secret.

SIR PETER TEAZLE. Eh? What the devil, Mr. Snake? Are you ashamed of having done a right thing for once in your life?

SNAKE. Sir, please understand, I live by the baseness of my character and if it were known that I had been persuaded into an honest act, even just once, I would lose every friend I have in the world.

SIR OLIVER SURFACE. Very well then, we'll not betray you by saying anything good about you.

SNAKE. A thousand thank-yous, sir. *(Snake makes elaborate flourish and leg, then exits, stage right.)*

SIR PETER TEAZLE. There goes a most perfect villain!

LADY TEAZLE. Sir Oliver, do you need further persuasion to consent to Charles and Maria's union?

SIR OLIVER SURFACE. I do not, madam. Egad, we shall have the wedding tomorrow morning, if you like.

LADY TEAZLE. And you, my dear husband, will you give your consent as well?

SIR PETER TEAZLE. With all my heart.

CHARLES SURFACE. Thank you, Sir Peter.

SIR OLIVER SURFACE. May your love last forever.

SIR PETER TEAZLE. And may you live as happily together as Lady Teazle and I intend to do!

CHARLES SURFACE. Rowley, dear old friend, I am sure I owe you a great deal.

SIR OLIVER SURFACE. You do, indeed, Charles.

SIR PETER TEAZLE. Ay, good Rowley always said you would reform.

CHARLES SURFACE. As to reforming, sir, I'll make no promises. *(To Maria.)* But here is my mentor and gentle guide. How could I ever leave the virtuous path these beautiful eyes illuminate? *(Kneeling and taking her hand.)* And even if thou, dear, sweet, Maria, shouldst ever give up thy command over me, thou will *still* rule my heart. I promise you this humble fugitive from folly will never seek any sanctuary but love and you. *(He rises. They kiss, then turn to the audience.)*

CHARLES SURFACE and MARIA. *(Together.)* You, too, can every anxious fear remove, for even scandal dies if you approve. *(The remaining actors onstage step to them and form a line, turning toward Charles and Maria. The order of the line-up is, from stage right to stage left: Rowley, Sir Oliver, Charles, Maria, Lady Teazle, Sir Peter. They take each other's hand, then together, to the audience, in their normal voices.)*

REMAINING CAST.
> For these sweet words you now do hear,
> We thanked and blessed our author dear.
> He smiled and said 'tis very clear,
> We should all play *deep* tragedy next year.

(Each actor now steps forward, in turn, to deliver the following lines:)

ROWLEY. Then drew he moral from this, his play,

MARIA. And with this counsel walked away:

CHARLES SURFACE. "Players, blessed are the wise like you, who stopped …

SIR OLIVER SURFACE. And ended folly, when the curtain dropped!
LADY TEAZLE. No more in vice or error to engage,
SIR PETER. Or play the fools at large ... on life's great stage."
(They take each other's hand and bow. The music begins and they are joined by the rest of the cast for applause and curtain calls.)

HERE ENDS THE PLAY

PROPERTY AND SET PIECES PLOT

PROLOGUE

Preset:
See ACT ONE, Scene 1 — Lady Sneerwell's Dressing Room

Hand props:
Factotum: staff

ACT ONE, Scene 1

Settee with cover
Dressing table with vanity tray, 2 perfume bottles, & hand mirror
Vanity tray contents: powder with puff, miscellaneous makeup, &
    jewelry box with necklace & miscellaneous jewelry
Dressing table stool
1 parlor chair
Square table with table cloth with Lady Sneerwell's wig on wig
    stand, jewelry box with jewelry, beauty marks in cloisonné
    box, & fan for Lady Sneerwell
Wall mirror
Small round "tea" table with table cloth & tea service
Tea service contents: tray with lace doily, 2 napkins, teapot,
    3 teacups with saucers & plate of sweets

Hand props:
Lady Sneerwell: Snake's "articles"
Snake: wrist handkerchief
Maria: fan & gloves
Mrs. Candor: fan
Sir Benjamin Backbite: lorgnette
Crabtree: walking stick

ACT ONE, Scene 2
Sir Peter's Parlor

Settee (without cover)
Long "settee" table with small vase of flowers & bell
Large round "drinks" table with tablecloth & silver drinks tray

Drinks tray contents: cognac decanter & 3 glasses
3 ladderback chairs
Square "flower" table with large vase of flowers

Hand props:
Sir Peter: flower shop bills

ACT ONE, Scene 3
Sir Peter's Parlor

Settee (without cover)
Long "settee" table with small vase of flowers & bell
Large round "drinks" table with tablecloth & silver drinks tray
Drinks tray contents: cognac decanter & 3 glasses
3 ladderback chairs
Square table with large vase of flowers
2 large floor flower arrangements in copper urns
2 columns with 2 large flower arrangements in white urns
2 large baskets filled with flowers

Hand props:
Lady Teazle: 1 stem of roses
Maid: fan, hat & gloves for Lady Teazle

ACT ONE, Scene 4
Lady Sneerwell's Parlor

Large round "drinks" table with tablecloth & silver drinks tray
Drinks tray contents: sherry decanter & 7 glasses
3 ladderback chairs with seat covers
Small round "game" table with deck of whist cards
2 parlor chairs

Hand props:
Lady Sneerwell: fan
Mrs. Candor: fan
Maria: fan & gloves
Lady Teazle: gloves & fan
Sir Benjamin Backbite: lorgnette & notebook
Crabtree: walking stick

ACT ONE, Scene 5
Sir Peter's Parlor

Settee (without cover)
Long "settee" table with large vase of flowers & bell
Large round "drinks" table with tablecloth & silver drinks tray
Drinks tray contents: cognac decanter & 3 glasses
3 ladderback chairs
Square "flower" table with small vase of flowers
2 large floor flower arrangements in copper urns
2 columns with 2 large flower arrangements in white urns
2 large baskets filled with flowers

Hand props:
George: luggage & packages
Mr. Premium: pocket watch
Maria: fan, hat & gloves
Sir Peter: 200 pounds
Lady Teazle: fan & satin purse

ACT ONE, Scene 6
Charles Surface's Dining Room

Large dining room table with tablecloth
2 benches
1 old chair
Bowl with 2 apples
2 tankards
6 wine bottles

Hand props:
Charles Surface: tankard
Sir Harry Bumper: tankard
Careless: tankard
A Gentleman: tankard
Mr. Premium: pocket watch
Sir Oliver: handkerchief

ACT ONE, Scene 7
Charles Surface's Picture Room

Long "podium" table with desktop podium & quill in inkpot
    family plaque
3 portrait paintings: Ravelin, Aunt Deborah & Sir Oliver

Hand props:
Charles: tankard
Sir Oliver: checkbook with loose check
Mr. Premium: pocket watch
Sir Harry Bumper: tankard & wine bottle

End ACT ONE — Intermission Speech

Hand props:
Factotum: staff

ACT TWO, Scene 1
Joseph Surface's Library

Long "books" table with 7 stacked books & hand mirror
Small round "drinks" table with silver drinks tray
Drinks tray contents: sherry decanter & 4 glasses
2 parlor chairs with seat covers
Wingback chair
Wingback side table with 3 books & candle in a candlestick
Square "hat" table
Screen & step stool

Hand props:
William: 3 books & candle
Lady Teazle: hat, gloves, fan & handkerchief
Sir Peter: walking stick & will
Sir Oliver: tricorn hat
Rowley: note

ACT TWO, Scene 2
Sir Peter's Parlor

Settee (without cover)
Long "settee" table with large vase of flowers & bell
Large round "drinks" table with tablecloth & silver drinks tray
Drinks tray contents: cognac decanter & 4 glasses
3 ladderback chairs
Square table with small vase of flowers

Hand props:
Mrs. Candor: fan
Lady Sneerwell: fan
Sir Benjamin Backbite: walking stick & lorgnette
Crabtree: walking stick
Sir Oliver: handkerchief
Rowley: handkerchief

ACT TWO, Scene 3
Joseph Surface's Library

Long "books" table with 7 stacked books & hand mirror
Small round "drinks" table with silver drinks tray
Drinks tray contents: sherry decanter & 4 glasses
2 parlor chairs with seat covers
Wingback chair
Wingback side table with 6 books & candle in a candlestick
Square "hat" table
Screen

Hand props:
Lady Sneerwell: fan
Sir Oliver: tricorn hat
Lady Teazle: fan
Maria: fan & gloves
Rowley: Sir Oliver's coat
Snake: wrist handkerchief & bundle of letters

MUSIC PLOT

Selections by Michael Nutt

AUDIENCE COMING IN
Finale, Theme and Variations
    from Divertimento in D .... Michael Haydn
Allegro assai, Allegro di Molto .... W.A. Mozart

OPENING OF PLAY, INTERRUPTED BY FACTOTUM
Air .... G.F. Handel

FACTOTUM EXIT MUSIC
Gigue .... G.F. Handel

BRIDGE TO SCENE TWO
March from Marriage of Figaro .... W.A. Mozart

BRIDGE TO SCENE THREE
Winter from The Four Seasons .... A. Vivaldi

BRIDGE TO SCENE FOUR
Bourree .... G.F. Handel

BRIDGE TO SCENE FIVE
Menuetto No. 1 .... A. Corelli

BRIDGE TO SCENE SIX
Corrente .... A. Corelli

BRIDGE TO SCENE SEVEN
Drinking Song .... Rick Ingrasci

BRIDGE TO FACTOTUM ENTRANCE
Bouree from Fireworks Music .... G.F. Handel

AUDIENCE OUT MUSIC
La Rejouissance .... G.F. Handel

SCENE CHANGE AT BEGINNING OF INTERMISSION
Finale, Theme and Variations
from Divertimento in D .... Michael Haydn

AUDIENCE COMES BACK IN, HOUSE LIGHTS DOWN
ACT TWO, SCENE ONE
Divertimento No. 1 .... W.A. Mozart

BRIDGE TO SCENE TWO
Concerto .... A. Vivaldi

BRIDGE TO SCENE THREE
Corrente, Vivace .... A. Corelli

MUSIC AT END OF PLAY
Hornpipe from Water Mask .... G.F. Handel

Sir Harry's Drinking Song

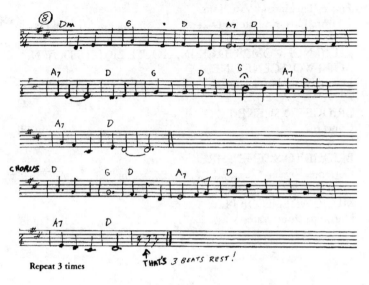

Repeat 3 times

THAT'S 3 BEATS REST!

Music by Rick Ingrasci

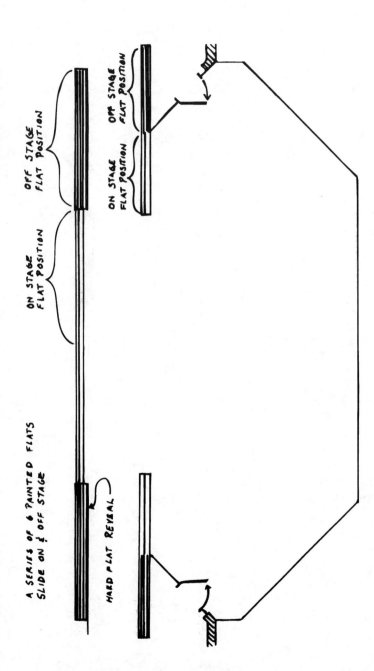

The School for Scandal   Set design by Sherri Brady

NEW PLAYS

★ **THE EXONERATED by Jessica Blank and Erik Jensen.** Six interwoven stories paint a picture of an American criminal justice system gone horribly wrong and six brave souls who persevered to survive it. "The #1 play of the year...intense and deeply affecting..." *–NY Times.* "Riveting. Simple, honest storytelling that demands reflection." *–A.P.* "Artful and moving...pays tribute to the resilience of human hearts and minds." *–Variety.* "Stark...riveting...cunningly orchestrated." *–The New Yorker.* "Hard-hitting, powerful, and socially relevant." *–Hollywood Reporter.* [7M, 3W] ISBN: 0-8222-1946-8

★ **STRING FEVER by Jacquelyn Reingold.** Lily juggles the big issues: turning forty, artificial insemination and the elusive scientific Theory of Everything in this Off-Broadway comedy hit. "Applies the elusive rules of string theory to the conundrums of one woman's love life. Think *Sex and the City* meets *Copenhagen.*" *–NY Times.* "A funny offbeat and touching look at relationships...an appealing romantic comedy populated by oddball characters." *–NY Daily News.* "Where kooky, zany, and madcap meet...whimsically winsome." *–NY Magazine.* "STRING FEVER will have audience members happily stringing along." *–TheaterMania.com.* "Reingold's language is surprising, inventive, and unique." *–nytheatre.com.* "...[a] whimsical comic voice." *–Time Out.* [3M, 3W (doubling)] ISBN: 0-8222-1952-2

★ **DEBBIE DOES DALLAS adapted by Erica Schmidt, composed by Andrew Sherman, conceived by Susan L. Schwartz.** A modern morality tale told as a comic musical of tragic proportions as the classic film is brought to the stage. "A scream! A saucy, tongue-in-cheek romp." *–The New Yorker.* "Hilarious! DEBBIE manages to have it all: beauty, brains and a great sense of humor!" *–Time Out.* "Shamelessly silly, shrewdly self-aware and proud of being naughty. Great fun!" *–NY Times.* "Racy and raucous, a lighthearted, fast-paced thoroughly engaging and hilarious send-up." *–NY Daily News.* [3M, 5W] ISBN: 0-8222-1955-7

★ **THE MYSTERY PLAYS by Roberto Aguirre-Sacasa.** Two interrelated one acts, loosely based on the tradition of the medieval mystery plays. "... stylish, spine-tingling...Mr. Aguirre-Sacasa uses standard tricks of horror stories, borrowing liberally from masters like Kafka, Lovecraft, Hitchcock...But his mastery of the genre is his own...irresistible." *–NY Times.* "Undaunted by the special-effects limitations of theatre, playwright and *Marvel* comic-book writer Roberto Aguirre-Sacasa maps out some creepy twilight zones in THE MYSTERY PLAYS, an engaging, related pair of one acts...The theatre may rarely deliver shocks equivalent to, say, *Dawn of the Dead*, but Aguirre-Sacasa's work is fine compensation." *–Time Out.* [4M, 2W] ISBN: 0-8222-2038-5

★ **THE JOURNALS OF MIHAIL SEBASTIAN by David Auburn.** This epic one-man play spans eight tumultuous years and opens a uniquely personal window on the Romanian Holocaust and the Second World War. "Powerful." *–NY Times.* "[THE JOURNALS OF MIHAIL SEBASTIAN] allows us to glimpse the idiosyncratic effects of that awful history on one intelligent, pragmatic, recognizably real man..." *–NY Newsday.* [3M, 5W] ISBN: 0-8222-2006-7

★ **LIVING OUT by Lisa Loomer.** The story of the complicated relationship between a Salvadoran nanny and the Anglo lawyer she works for. "A stellar new play. Searingly funny." *–The New Yorker.* "Both generous and merciless, equally enjoyable and disturbing." *–NY Newsday.* "A bitingly funny new comedy. The plight of working mothers is explored from two pointedly contrasting perspectives in this sympathetic, sensitive new play." *–Variety.* [2M, 6W] ISBN: 0-8222-1994-8

DRAMATISTS PLAY SERVICE, INC.
440 Park Avenue South, New York, NY 10016 212-683-8960 Fax 212-213-1539
postmaster@dramatists.com www.dramatists.com

NEW PLAYS

★ **MATCH by Stephen Belber.** Mike and Lisa Davis interview a dancer and choreographer about his life, but it is soon evident that their agenda will either ruin or inspire them—and definitely change their lives forever. "Prolific laughs and ear-to-ear smiles." *–NY Magazine.* "Uproariously funny, deeply moving, enthralling theater. Stephen Belber's MATCH has great beauty and tenderness, and abounds in wit." *–NY Daily News.* "Three and a half out of four stars." *–USA Today.* "A theatrical steeplechase that leads straight from outrageous bitchery to unadorned, heartfelt emotion." *–Wall Street Journal.* [2M, 1W] ISBN: 0-8222-2020-2

★ **HANK WILLIAMS: LOST HIGHWAY by Randal Myler and Mark Harelik.** The story of the beloved and volatile country-music legend Hank Williams, featuring twenty-five of his most unforgettable songs. "[LOST HIGHWAY has] the exhilarating feeling of Williams on stage in a particular place on a particular night…serves up classic country with the edges raw and the energy hot…By the end of the play, you've traveled on a profound emotional journey: LOST HIGHWAY transports its audience and communicates the inspiring message of the beauty and richness of Williams' songs…forceful, clear-eyed, moving, impressive." *–Rolling Stone.* "…honors a very particular musical talent with care and energy… smart, sweet, poignant." *–NY Times.* [7M, 3W] ISBN: 0-8222-1985-9

★ **THE STORY by Tracey Scott Wilson.** An ambitious black newspaper reporter goes against her editor to investigate a murder and finds the *best* story…but at what cost? "A singular new voice…deeply emotional, deeply intellectual, and deeply musical…" *–The New Yorker.* "…a conscientious and absorbing new drama…" *–NY Times.* "…a riveting, tough-minded drama about race, reporting and the truth…" *–A.P.* "… a stylish, attention-holding script that ends on a chilling note that will leave viewers with much to talk about." *–Curtain Up.* [2M, 7W (doubling, flexible casting)] ISBN: 0-8222-1998-0

★ **OUR LADY OF 121st STREET by Stephen Adly Guirgis.** The body of Sister Rose, beloved Harlem nun, has been stolen, reuniting a group of life-challenged childhood friends who square off as they wait for her return. "A scorching and dark new comedy… Mr. Guirgis has one of the finest imaginations for dialogue to come along in years." *–NY Times.* "Stephen Guirgis may be the best playwright in America under forty." *–NY Magazine.* [8M, 4W] ISBN: 0-8222-1965-4

★ **HOLLYWOOD ARMS by Carrie Hamilton and Carol Burnett.** The coming-of-age story of a dreamer who manages to escape her bleak life and follow her romantic ambitions to stardom. Based on Carol Burnett's bestselling autobiography, *One More Time.* "…pure theatre and pure entertainment…" *–Talkin' Broadway.* "…a warm, fuzzy evening of theatre." *–BrodwayBeat.com.* "…chuckles and smiles of recognition or surprise flow naturally…a remarkable slice of life." *–TheatreScene.net.* [5M, 5W, 1 girl] ISBN: 0-8222-1959-X

★ **INVENTING VAN GOGH by Steven Dietz.** A haunting and hallucinatory drama about the making of art, the obsession to create and the fine line that separates truth from myth. "Like a van Gogh painting, Dietz's story is a gorgeous example of excess—one that remakes reality with broad, well-chosen brush strokes. At evening's end, we're left with the author's resounding opinions on art and artifice, and provoked by his constant query into which is greater: van Gogh's art or his violent myth." *–Phoenix New Times.* "Dietz's writing is never simple. It is always brilliant. Shaded, compressed, direct, lucid—he frames his subject with a remarkable understanding of painting as a physical experience." *–Tucson Citizen.* [4M, 1W] ISBN: 0-8222-1954-9

DRAMATISTS PLAY SERVICE, INC.
440 Park Avenue South, New York, NY 10016   212-683-8960   Fax 212-213-1539
postmaster@dramatists.com   www.dramatists.com

NEW PLAYS

★ **INTIMATE APPAREL by Lynn Nottage.** The moving and lyrical story of a turn-of-the-century black seamstress whose gifted hands and sewing machine are the tools she uses to fashion her dreams from the whole cloth of her life's experiences. "...Nottage's play has a delicacy and eloquence that seem absolutely right for the time she is depicting..." –*NY Daily News.* "...thoughtful, affecting...The play offers poignant commentary on an era when the cut and color of one's dress—and of course, skin—determined whom one could and could not marry, sleep with, even talk to in public." –*Variety.* [2M, 4W] ISBN: 0-8222-2009-1

★ **BROOKLYN BOY by Donald Margulies.** A witty and insightful look at what happens to a writer when his novel hits the bestseller list. "The characters are beautifully drawn, the dialogue sparkles..." –*nytheatre.com.* "Few playwrights have the mastery to smartly investigate so much through a laugh-out-loud comedy that combines the vintage subject matter of successful writer-returning-to-ethnic-roots with the familiar mid-life crisis." –*Show Business Weekly.* [4M, 3W] ISBN: 0-8222-2074-1

★ **CROWNS by Regina Taylor.** Hats become a springboard for an exploration of black history and identity in this celebratory musical play. "Taylor pulls off a Hat Trick: She scores thrice, turning CROWNS into an artful amalgamation of oral history, fashion show, and musical theater..." –*TheatreMania.com.* "...wholly theatrical...Ms. Taylor has created a show that seems to arise out of spontaneous combustion, as if a bevy of department-store customers simultaneously decided to stage a revival meeting in the changing room." –*NY Times.* [1M, 6W (2 musicians)] ISBN: 0-8222-1963-8

★ **EXITS AND ENTRANCES by Athol Fugard.** The story of a relationship between a young playwright on the threshold of his career and an aging actor who has reached the end of his. "[Fugard] can say more with a single line than most playwrights convey in an entire script...Paraphrasing the title, it's safe to say this drama, making its memorable entrance into our consciousness, is unlikely to exit as long as a theater exists for exceptional work." –*Variety.* "A thought-provoking, elegant and engrossing new play..." –*Hollywood Reporter.* [2M] ISBN: 0-8222-2041-5

★ **BUG by Tracy Letts.** A thriller featuring a pair of star-crossed lovers in an Oklahoma City motel facing a bug invasion, paranoia, conspiracy theories and twisted psychological motives. "...obscenely exciting...top-flight craftsmanship. Buckle up and brace yourself..." –*NY Times.* "...[a] thoroughly outrageous and thoroughly entertaining play...the possibility of enemies, real and imagined, to squash has never been more theatrical." –*A.P.* [3M, 2W] ISBN: 0-8222-2016-4

★ **THOM PAIN (BASED ON NOTHING) by Will Eno.** An ordinary man muses on childhood, yearning, disappointment and loss, as he draws the audience into his last-ditch plea for empathy and enlightenment. "It's one of those treasured nights in the theater—treasured nights anywhere, for that matter—that can leave you both breathless with exhilaration and...in a puddle of tears." –*NY Times.* "Eno's words...are familiar, but proffered in a way that is constantly contradictory to our expectations. Beckett is certainly among his literary ancestors." –*nytheatre.com.* [1M] ISBN: 0-8222-2076-8

★ **THE LONG CHRISTMAS RIDE HOME by Paula Vogel.** Past, present and future collide on a snowy Christmas Eve for a troubled family of five. "...[a] lovely and hauntingly original family drama...a work that breathes so much life into the theater." –*Time Out.* "...[a] delicate visual feast..." –*NY Times.* "...brutal and lovely...the overall effect is magical." –*NY Newsday.* [3M, 3W] ISBN: 0-8222-2003-2

DRAMATISTS PLAY SERVICE, INC.
440 Park Avenue South, New York, NY 10016 212-683-8960 Fax 212-213-1539
postmaster@dramatists.com   www.dramatists.com